FCB-ULKA
BRAND
BUILDING
ADVERTISING
Concepts and Cases

FCB-ULKA
BRAND
BUILDING
ADVERTISING
Concepts and Cases

M G Parameswaran
Executive Director
FCB-Ulka Advertising Ltd.
Mumbai

Tata McGraw-Hill Publishing Company Limited
NEW DELHI

McGraw-Hill Offices

New Delhi New York St Louis San Francisco Auckland Bogotá
Caracas Kuala Lumpur Lisbon London Madrid Mexico City Milan
Montreal San Juan Santiago Singapore Sydney Tokyo Toronto

Tata McGraw-Hill
*A Division of The **McGraw·Hill** Companies*

© 2001, Tata McGraw-Hill Publishing Company Limited

No part of this publication and the companion CD can be reproduced in any form or by any means without the prior written permission of the publishers

This edition can be exported from India only by the publishers,
Tata McGraw-Hill Publishing Company Limited

ISBN 0-07-463338-4

Published by Tata McGraw-Hill Publishing Company Limited,
7 West Patel Nagar, New Delhi 110 008, typeset at Anvi Composers, A-1/33,
Paschim Vihar, New Delhi 110 063 and printed at Gopson Papers Limited,
A-28, Sector IX Noida

Cover Design: Kam Studio

RZACRRXLLZBLB

Preface

This book has been designed to provide a snapshot view of various advertising situations faced by Indian marketers. The primary focus is on providing a young professional or a management student an overview of the complex marketing–advertising situations.

The book is based on actual cases—brands handled by FCB-Ulka Advertising. Given the paucity of case study material in the Indian context, the book is an attempt to add to the literature available for training and teaching purposes.

In order to give a conceptual framework, each section is preceded by a 'concept' chapter. This is by no means an elaborate analysis of 'how advertising works' or 'how to create advertising'. At best, these chapters provide a concise methodology for approaching each product–market situation.

The concept chapters have used the legendary FCB Grid as a template. While theoretical knowledge of 'how advertising works' is growing and many more models have been developed, FCB Grid still has its appeal.

The book is organised into six sections:

- Consumer Products
- Consumer Durables
- Services
- Corporate
- Rural Inputs
- Beyond Brands

While it is true that fundamental marketing concepts do not change, it is often useful to understand the nuances of each marketing situation. Our sincere effort here has been to provide the young professional a wider exposure through these myriad cases.

■ In order to make the book more reader friendly, and to demystify the marketing–advertising processes, the book offers several additional features:

■ '*Infoline*' sections scattered throughout the book provide interesting insights into Indian markets and consumers. These have been derived from various published sources.

■ '*They Said So*' include quotes from leading thinkers on marketing and advertising. Hopefully, these will inspire the young reader to go to the original publications, from where these quotes have been derived.

■ '*Heard-in-the-Agency*' are humorous anecdotes based on actual exchanges heard in an agency (cartoons have been done by Subash Tendle, Creative Director at FCB-Ulka).

■ '*Query Line*' are multiple-choice questions with answers included at various points of the book. These have been extensively used by FCB-Ulka as a part of the Management Trainee selection programme. A young student could learn a few trade tricks from these questions.

 ■ '*Companion CD*' contains the successful print and television ad campaigns on brand building.

An attempt has been made to make the book wholesome and fun to read, while being educational and informative at the same time. It is hoped that this book will aid and spur additional efforts to add to 'real-life' case material for young students and professionals.

M G PARAMESWARAN

Acknowledgements

The credit for the book goes to the great team of advertising professionals at FCB-Ulka Advertising. Without their active support and help, this book would have remained a pipe dream. Several cases were co-authored by them and several others were intensely critiqued and discussed.

The book would also have been impossible without the active support of our clients. I wish to place on record, and convey to all the clients whose case studies have been reproduced in this book, my sincere gratitude and appreciation. With due deference to confidentiality needs of the clients and the data relating to their products, I have taken the necessary care and caution not to divulge any information relating to the clients or their brands which are not already in the public domain. The stated case studies are based on factual data and developments, shortcomings, if any, in the reproduction of the case studies are unintended.

Ms V Deepa of Tata McGraw-Hill has my sincere gratitude. Without her enthusiasm and follow ups, the book would have taken much more time to reach your hands.

Finally my overriding debt to my wife Nithya and my son Aditya for all those holidays and Sundays which were taken up by this book. I gratefully dedicate this book to them and to the FCB-Ulka team who have made this book possible.

M G PARAMESWARAN

Contents

Introduction

"Advertising is nothing but salesmanship in print."
• **John Kennedy 1904**
Copywriter

The story goes that one day Albert Lasker, who was the head of the advertising agency Lord & Thomas, received a note from a young man that said, 'I know the secret of great advertising. To find out more, meet me at the diner next door'. Much amused, Albert Lasker, then one of the biggest names in American advertising, went over to the diner to meet the young man. This young man was John Kennedy, who told Albert Lasker that 'Advertising is salesmanship in print'. Albert Lasker hired the young man who went on to become one of the biggest names in advertising, making Lord & Thomas America's number one advertising agency. Did everything change or was it a mere play of words?

Till the term 'salesmanship in print' was coined, advertising was seen as 'information dissemination'. The manufacturer and the advertising agent communicated the facts about a product and the consumer rushed out and bought the product. Simple.

'Salesmanship' added a whole new dimension to the advertising process. Ads could now 'sell'. Ads needed to use all the fine persuasive skills of a salesman to sell. The art of persuasion in advertising was unleashed and advertising has never been the same again.

ADVERTISING TODAY

Today advertising has taken a quantum leap beyond just salesmanship of products in print. It is the art of persuasion of human minds through a whole range of communication media. The bottom line of advertising is to sell by creating positive impressions about a product, service or a concept. Advertising today ranges from the basics like selling salt to the most abstract like selling polio vaccination.

Brand Building

Management thinkers today strongly believe that the customer is king. The single most important job in marketing is the job of creating and retaining a customer. Numerous research studies across the world have proven that the best way of creating and retaining customers is by building strong brands. Now what are brands? Products? Enhanced products? Products with names? In a simple equation:

$$\boxed{\text{Brand} = \text{Product} + \text{Images}}$$

A brand is more, much more than the mere product it stands for. A brand is the amalgam of the physical product and the notional images that go with the brand. When we recall a brand, not only do we recall the physicality of the product but also the images it conjures.

Sundrop	= *Sunflower Oil + (Healthy family + Happy Children + Loving Mother + Tasty Food + Modern Home + ...)*
LML Vespa	= *Scooter + (Style + Extra Power + Macho Image + Great Looks + International)*
Godrej Storwel	= *Steel Cupboard + (Lasting Value + Premium + Care + Family Heirloom....)*

Salesmanship to Brand Building

The hub of advertising today is to go beyond mere selling. Advertising has to create those positive images that linger in the consumer's mind and lead to 'brand' building. Advertising that only sells will end up, in today's market environment, merely creating commodity brands. The task of advertising today, therefore, is to sell and simultaneously endow the brand with all those positive values that will make it more attractive to the target consumers.

HOW TO CREATE BRAND BUILDING ADVERTISING?

The global market place is littered with skeletons of brands that died too soon. The Indian market is no exception. For instance if one were to count the failures in categories like soaps alone, the number would be incredibly high. But is it all due to advertising? Well not fully. However, advertising could have saved a number of those brands by resorting to focussed 'brand building advertising', because it is the kind of advertising that sells today and builds enduring brand values over time.

Brand building advertising is not an accident or a mere fluke. It is an orchestrated attempt to use the right processes and procedures by a team of well-trained people, of total teamwork with the other agency teams (servicing, creative, planning, media) and client teams (brand management, development etc.).

Brand building is a result of this teamwork and understanding. Brand building advertising is the right blend of 'sell' and 'build value', the yin and yang of advertising. This calls for a lot of patience and understanding from clients, and for sustained hard work and creative efforts from the agency team.

ADVERTISING PROCESS: GUIDELINES

Advertising is an element of the marketing mix and hence advertising objectives are derived *per se* from the organisation's marketing objectives. From objectives we move on to advertising strategy and advertising execution. But great advertising often needs the agency to go back several stages. Back to the base camp. To level zero.

Better advertising is born out of a total understanding of all the variables impacting the brand. It may be new consumer trends, new competition, or new technological breakthroughs.

Brand building advertising is created only after a cohesive interface between the A-B-C-D-E of analysis. Such advertising is often right on strategy. But great advertising gives strategy the golden glow of creativity. The skin care benefit gets the golden glow of 'mistaken identity'

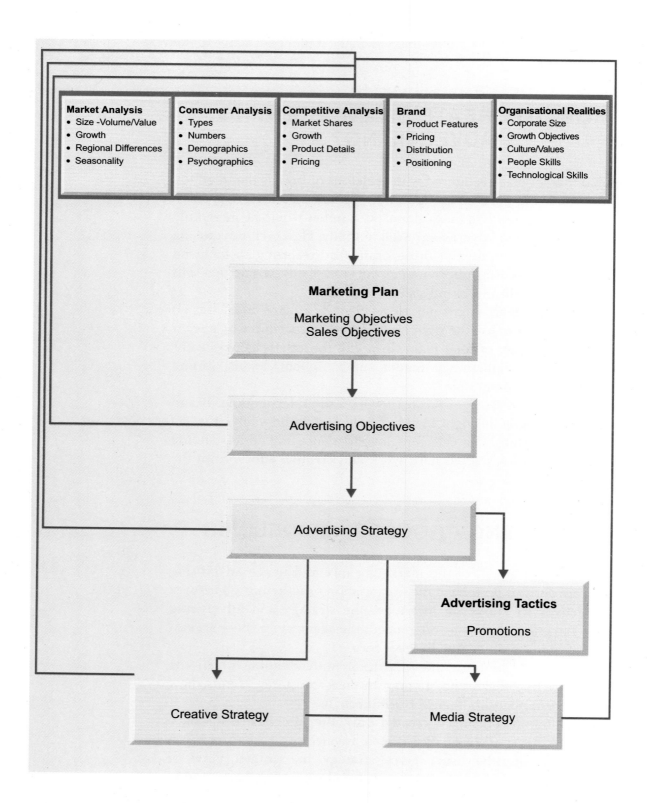

Market Analysis	Consumer Analysis	Competitive Analysis	Brand	Organisational Realities
• Size -Volume/Value • Growth • Regional Differences • Seasonality	• Types • Numbers • Demographics • Psychographics	• Market Shares • Growth • Product Details • Pricing	• Product Features • Pricing • Distribution • Positioning	• Corporate Size • Growth Objectives • Culture/Values • People Skills • Technological Skills

Marketing Plan

Marketing Objectives
Sales Objectives

Advertising Objectives

Advertising Strategy

Advertising Tactics

Promotions

Creative Strategy

Media Strategy

in 'Santoor'. The largest size gets the golden glow of 'no machine can wash so many' in Voltas.

REFERENCES

- Claude C Hopkins: *My life in Advertising and Scientific Advertising* (in one volume) (Chicago: Crain Books, 1996)
- Kotler, Philip: Marketing Management (Prentice-Hall of India Pvt. Ltd., 1999)
- Ries, Al and Jack Trout: *Positioning: The Battle for Your Mind* (Warner Books by arrangement with McGraw-Hill Book Company, 1980)
- Aaker, David A, Rajeev Batra and John G Myers: *Advertising Management* (Prentice-Hall of India, Ltd. 1996)
- Vaughn, Richard: "How Advertising works—A Planning Model" *Journal of Advertising Research,* 20, 5 (1980)
- Jones, John Philip: *What's in a Brand* (Tata McGraw-Hill Publishing Company Ltd., 1998)
- Bogart, Leo: *Strategy in Advertising* (Chicago: Grain Books, 1984)
- Levitt, Theodore: *The Marketing Imagination* (New York: Free Press, 1983)

Brand Building Consumer Product Advertising

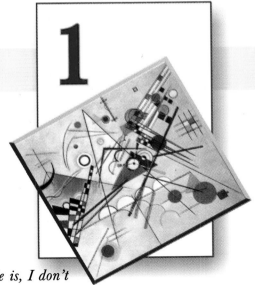

"Half my advertising is wasted—the trouble is, I don't know which half".
• **Lord Leverhume**

*L*ord Leverhume's words would probably go down in history as the most over-used words about the nebulous nature of advertising. The role of advertising in brand building is put to the ultimate test in the case of consumer products.

CONSUMER PRODUCTS

The term consumer products or FMCG (Fast Moving Consumer Goods) is used to describe a whole range of products that are 'consumed' by consumers, in some form or the other. The products here range from the lowly salt to exalted perfumes, from wheat flour to shampoos, from soaps to pickles.

By definition consumer products are bought by consumers at regular intervals, almost like clockwork. Also, product differentiation is the least in the case of consumer products. A soap is a soap. If this is the case, why should a consumer choose a particular brand, and stick to it month after month?

In the case of consumer products, our brand equation will probably read as:

Brand = Product + Image

How Does Advertising Work?

Foote, Cone & Belding, America's number one agency, did pioneering work in the 1970s to understand how advertising works, to build brands, for both consumer products and durables. The model they developed has been much written about as the FCB Grid.

The model proposes that consumers have different degrees of involvement with their product/brand purchases and we can categorise them as 'high' and 'low'. For instance, in the Indian setting, salt implies low involvement while cooking oil implies high involvement. Further, the model suggests that consumers do not always act rationally. Their behaviour is often a mix of rational (thinking) and emotional (feeling) reasons. For instance, the purchase of a soft drink is going to be dictated more by feelings than thinking and the case is just the opposite in the case of, say, a detergent powder. The model went on to suggest that depending on the product type we can fine tune our advertising to work harder.

	Thinking	Feeling
High Involvement	I Informative	II Affective
Low Involvement	III Habitual	IV Satisfaction

Applying the grid to the Indian context we could slot products into broad quadrants:

    I : Automobiles, TVs

   II : Perfumes, Cosmetics

  III : Pain balms, Detergents

   IV : Confectionery

Often it makes sense to look at the quadrant, see what kind of advertising would work, look at competitive advertising and then decide the path to follow. At times, brands have been built by going just about a little 'off centre' and stretching the limit.

Brand Building Advertising

Consumer product advertising is probably the most researched form of advertising. It also eminently makes sense to research it thoroughly since in no other product does advertising comprise such a large part of investment. However, it is necessary to research advertising for consumer products with a lot more sensitivity. Often we are dealing with 'feelings' and human emotions. Unless we are careful, it is likely that great brand building advertising would get rejected by a group of women sitting in a room, sipping tea in a remote town like Muzzafarpur.

The usual process of advertising testing in consumer products is lengthy and often well-documented.

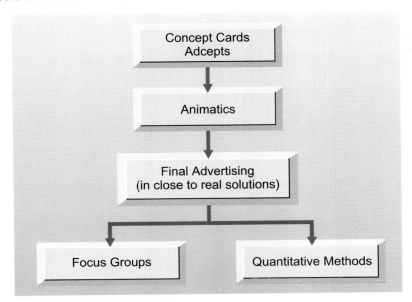

A large part of consumer product advertising today is on television. This makes testing all the more difficult. However much you try, you can never create the magic of the final commercial in a 'ripomatic' or an 'animatic' story board. Hence each brand needs its own advertising 'look and feel'. Research, at best, will give vital clues on how consumers will react to the final commercial.

BRAND TRACKING

In no other product category can one 'track' brand equities as well as one can in consumer products. This is probably because in India customised/ off-the-shelf brand trading studies are available primarily for consumer products. Further, given the parity status across brands, the brand tracking studies give a marketeer and the agency a reading of brand health and potential. While brand tracking studies are important across any brand advertising, they are of major importance in consumer products, for the reasons mentioned above. Brand tracks help keep a track of the brand in the key consumers' minds covering:

- Top of the Mind Awareness
- Unaided Awareness
- Current Usage
- Brand Image Scores Across
- Product Dimensions
- Benefit Dimensions
- Personality Dimension

CASES

The following section consists of four cases covering a range of consumer product brands. Each case is an example of brand building advertising, from level zero. In fact, one case is an example of turnaround advertising while another covers umbrella branding.

SANTOOR: Success more than skin deep

BACKGROUND

The Indian soap market is probably the most competitive market in the FMCG arena. For every brand that succeeds in this market, there are at least 10–15 brands that have failed to make an impact. At the centre of all this is the consumer, who is watching all of it with interest, buying one brand today and another one the next month, appearing to be seduced by a new promise, a new offer, a new ingredient, a new hope. However, below the surface, the consumer is extremely stable, promising loyalty to his favourite brands, for a considerable length of time.

The soap market is divided into three broad segments—Premium, Popular and Economy. The total market was estimated at 420,000 tonnes per annum (TPA) or Rs 27,000 million (MM) in the year 1995. The market, in tonnage terms was growing at a healthy 5 + per cent per annum. The market consisted of over 100 brands from 20 odd companies but a handful of companies such as Hindustan Lever, Godrej, Swastik, Colgate Palmolive and Nirma dominated the market.

The rural consumer accounted for almost 40 per cent of the total volume and that segment was growing at a much higher rate.

The Soap Market Pyramid (1995)

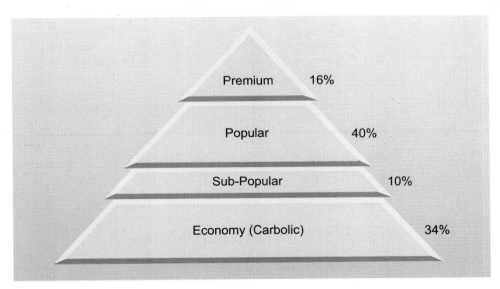

COMPETITION

While the market consisted of over 100 brands, a handful of brands dominated the market. Most of them had a long history in the country and were supported by big companies with large promotional budgets.

In the economy segment, the giant brand was Lifebuoy. This brand cut across the entire country with its promise of 'health'. With a strong franchise in rural areas and lower income segments in urban areas, the brand virtually controlled the economy segment. The other notable brand in this segment included Nirma Bath and TOMCO's OK. Neither of these had been able to make a serious dent on Lifebuoy.

The Popular segment consisted of a number of established brands including Lux, Rexona, Hamam, etc. Each of these brands offered a strong benefit to the consumer and had occupied a distinct position in the consumers' mind. Nirma Beauty was making waves with its lower price– better value offering, in this segment.

The Premium segment consisted of a number of brands with smaller volumes. However, the key players in this segment were Cinthol, Lux International, Palmolive, Margo, Liril and Mysore Sandal. This segment had attracted a lot of interest in the 1980s with a spate of new brand launches from large companies. Many of these brands like Ponds, Lakme and Clearasil failed to make an impact on the Indian premium soap consumer.

■ Table 1.1 Brand—Benefit Analysis

Brand	Segment	Benefit	Support
Lifebuoy	Economy	Health	Germ kill
Lux	Popular	Beauty	Film stars
Rexona	Popular	Skin	Coconut oil
Hamam	Popular	Health	Purity
Cinthol	Premium	Deodoriser	Ingredient
Liril	Premium	Freshness	Lime
Palmolive	Premium	Skin	Moisturisers

The soap marketeers were one of the most aggressive advertisers/promoters spending over Rs 780 million on advertising in 1985.

WIPRO'S NEW ENTRY: SANTOOR

In 1985, sensing an opportunity in the popular soap segment, Wipro introduced a sandalwood-turmeric based soap called 'Santoor'. The

INDIA—A PROFILE

How big is India? What do Indian households buy? Where are they located? The National Council of Applied Economic Research (NCAER) has been doing seminal work in this area. The study published in 1996, covering consumption and ownership of durables and non-durables, also projected income levels into the next millennium.

Households have been categorised into five classes:

The Destitutes	:	Annual Household Income (AHI) of up to Rs 16,000
The Aspirants	:	AHI of Rs 16,001 to Rs 22,000
The Climbers	:	AHI of Rs 22,001 to Rs 45,000
The Consuming Class	:	AHI of Rs 45,001 to Rs 2,15,000
The Very Rich	:	AHI of Rs 2,15,001 and above

The study presents the number of such households across the country—urban and rural, as of 1994-95.

(Nos in millions)

	Rural	Urban	Total
The Very Rich	0.3	0.70	1.00
The Consuming Class	14.3	14.3	28.6
The Climbers	32.7	15.3	48.0
The Aspirants	39.7	8.3	48.0
The Destitutes	28.9	6.1	35.0
Total	115.9	44.7	160.6

In absolute numbers India is an awesome market, with over 160 million households. But a closer look reveals the real potential.

For most mass market consumer products, the real market is just about 80 million households. If we were to look at the market for luxury products, the market is just about 1 million households...

But the good news is that by the year 2006-07, these numbers are expected to rise significantly. The very rich will number in excess of 5 million! The consuming class will number over 75 million households!

Till that day dawns, the premium luxury products will have to cater to a small microcosm of the Indian society—often referred to as the 'Churchgate Set' in Bombay!

Source: Business Today, April 7–21, 1997

company had earlier tested seven product concepts out of which the sandalwood-turmeric concept emerged as the winner. The product was unique and relevant due to the 'skin care' and 'beauty' benefits it offered. Traditionally, sandalwood and turmeric paste have been used for their beautifying properties. Santoor offered all the benefits of sandalwood and turmeric while doing away with the time-consuming and cumbersome process of making the paste. The brand name, 'Santoor', was derived from the first three letters of both the ingredients 'san'dalwood + 'tur'meric.

Santoor was test marketed in Bangalore in late 1985. Priced at Rs 3.00 + local taxes at a premium of Rs 0.10 over Lux, for a 100 gm pack, Santoor was positioned as a 'sandal & turmeric' beauty soap at a reasonable price. At this point of time, Moti and Mysore Sandal were the only other sandal-based soaps available, but both were in the premium category. Brand performance was closely monitored and the results were encouraging. Findings indicated that the basic concept was seen as unique and strong, and both the brand name and the packaging were well-liked. The advertising, which used "goodness of sandal and turmeric in a soap" story was found to be far too traditional. Consumers also wanted the fragrance/perfume to be strengthened.

Based on the feedback, the brand mix was suitably modified. Advertising was changed to make it more contemporary, the focus on the ingredients increased and the perfume/fragrance was strengthened.

The brand was launched in the west and other markets in the south. Consumer and trade acceptance was good. A shortage of Lux at this point of time helped the brand and it was identified as a success with brand sales of 1500 TPA (tonnes per annum) and an all India market share of 1.5 per cent.

They Said So

"....the organisation must learn to think of itself not as producing goods or services but as buying customers, as doing the things that will make people want to do business with it."

• **Theodore Levitt,**
"Marketing Myopia"
Harvard Business Review (July–August 1960)

SANTOOR: Phase II

1987 was a turbulent period for the soap industry in general and Santoor in particular. The cost of vegetable oils, that make for the total fatty matter (T.F.M) which determines the lathering ability, spiralled. This was accompanied by an increase in packaging cost and the imposition of excise duties, which made matters worse. The prices of all popular soaps increased by more than a rupee.

Santoor was severely affected by the increased prices. Consumers switched from Santoor to the lower priced brands and other new brands introduced at lower price band. Being a relatively new brand, Santoor had not yet built the required brand loyalty to retain consumers, who felt that the price hikes were unjustified. To counter this, a new campaign highlighting 'beauty care and VFM (value for money)' was developed.

The year after was fairly stable in terms of prices. Santoor had improved and extended its distribution network and to some extent, had partially recovered from the setback it suffered. Volumes stabilised at around 2,400 TPA. The brand, however, was not making much headway in the marketplace due to heavy competitive pressures.

Wipro felt that Santoor was onto a good thing and that the brand had the potential to grow. The problem, however, was that new consumers were not entering Santoor's fold. Due to the competitive nature of the market, boredom was setting in, resulting in consumer shifts to other new brands and a decline in trial rate.

Heard-in-the-Agency

(Amusing exchanges between 'anxious' servicing and even more 'anxious' creative folks.)

"I'm just an Assistant A.E., 22 years old, just out of Business School, not a writer, but somehow I don't feel your copy is as crisp as it could be. It just doesn't... sing. You're not upset, are you?"

In 1989, FCB-Ulka was appointed and entrusted with the responsibility of building Santoor as a strong brand. The brief was clear and direct. Double the sales volumes from 2,400 TPA to approximately 5000 TPA and increase TOM awareness levels from 0.8 per cent to at least 4.5 per cent.

Faced with this task, the agency examined the problem from various angles. Why are some brands more successful than others? Is it because of a better product? Do they create new segments? Or is it the advertising? The conclusion was that the product quality of the brand was good, and if product quality alone was the determinant, then Santoor would not have found itself in the problem it was in.

Talking to the Consumer

The agency carried out research to determine the consumers' attitude to Santoor and beauty soaps in general. The study was conducted among

600 respondents in Cochin and Bombay and reactions were obtained on various parameters ranging from functional to image.

Findings indicated that a low correlation existed between the brand name and the ingredient story. There was low excitement around the brand. The brand had a middle class image and no strong benefit was highlighted in the communication.

Research also showed that Santoor appealed only to a small set of users who wanted a sandalwood-based soap. Outside this set, it had no 'brand equity' whatsoever. Santoor had become a niche brand in a mass market, catering to a very small user base.

Other findings regarding consumer expectations revealed that the consumer wanted a soap that was 'good for the skin'. Fragrance, 'price', 'lathers well', 'has a long life', 'colour', 'shape', were the other parameters on which Santoor scored very well.

Other interesting findings were that women liked to be admired and loved, that beauty and good looks were desirable attributes and that there was a positive relationship between looking good and the soap.

Important cultural changes were taking place as well. The consumer taste was moving from traditional to modern lifestyles—a trend seen in other product categories as well, due to increasing urbanisation and rise in disposable incomes. People were taking more care in the way they dressed and looked and the image they projected. Concern with beauty, looking good was on the rise and there was greater emphasis on self (I) than before.

Against this background, Santoor was seen as a traditional middle class brand and the spokesperson, the Santoor woman, was neither noticed nor looked up to.

The Quandary

The soap market being a highly competitive market, Santoor had to retain its traditional users (who accounted for 2400 TPA), while going after new users. The brand had to continue offering the same value to its users while presenting a new face to the non-users. How could it do this?

Positioning

Santoor as a brand offered two useful 'ingredients' (sandal +turmeric) to consumers. It was priced attractively and the soap's product characteristics (lathering, fragrance, post-bath feel) were well appreciated. The brand, however, offered no 'benefit' to the consumer.

A product ingredient analysis revealed that both sandal and turmeric were proven to be very good skin care ingredients. Indian women have been using sandalwood paste and turmeric as skin care ingredients for many centuries. The question was: can we focus on something more than just 'good skin' or 'skin care'?

Here again literature analysis revealed that these ingredients can help in keeping the skin tight and supple, leading to the breakthrough thought, 'younger looking skin'.

Santoor was positioned as a soap that offers 'younger looking skin'. The ingredients sandal and turmeric were to be used as a strong support for the 'younger looking' proposition.

In addition to positioning Santoor in a realm that would appeal to the consumer, it was also decided that the brand had to break away from its middle class lineage and start moving, at least a bit, into a more modern milieu.

The creative team was given the challenge to break out of the soap advertising clutter and create a unique property for Santoor, that would build sales and brand equity over time.

Santoor Brand Profile

Santoor	Before	After
Ingredients	Sandal + Turmeric	Sandal + Turmeric
Price	Value - Popular	Value - Popular
Benefit	Skin ?	Skin
- Specific	?	Younger Looking Skin
Appeal	Traditional	Modern - Progressive

Creative Execution

Santoor had to be positioned as a "good for skin–younger looking skin" soap with a strong ingredient support from sandal and turmeric. The creative teams got to work to generate numerous ideas. These were then converted into animatics or storyboards for further consumer testing.

The final execution that won the day was based on the creative insight of 'mistaken identity'. It was found that the most identifiable way of

Santoor–Bookshop

Film opens on a bookshop where the Santoor woman is searching for a book.
Sound Effects: Music

Cut to small girl emerging from one corner of the shop shouting "Mummy".

Cut to ingredient shot of turmeric and sandal.
Jingle: Filled with the goodness of turmeric and sandal.

Cut to two other girls who spot the Santoor woman and start moving towards her.
Sound Effects: Music

Cut to the Santoor woman and the kid hugging each other and both of them laughing.
Sound Effects: Music

Cut to pack shot of Santoor soap.
Jingle: Making life more beautiful.

One of the two girls asks the Santoor woman. Excuse me, which college do you study in?

Cut to close-up of the Santoor woman. Santoor woman: This usually happens. My skin never gives away my age.

Film ends with the close-up shot of the Santoor woman and the kid.
Jingle: Santoor... Santoor
Super: Making life more beautiful.

Santoor–Wedding

Film opens on the Santoor woman at a traditional Indian wedding.
Sound Effects: Music

Cut to the elderly women.
Lady: Why don't we get this girl married to our Raju?

Cut to ingredient shot of turmeric and sandal.
Jingle: Filled with the goodness of turmeric

Cut to two elderly women looking at the girl and commenting. Look how beautiful and cheerful she looks.

Cut to a little girl emerging from one corner of the wedding hall.
Girl: Mummy

Cut to pack shot of Santoor soap.
Jingle continues: ... Making life more beautiful.

Cut to close-up of the Santoor woman who overhears this and laughs.

Look of surprise on the elderly woman's faces.
Santoor Girl speaking: It always happens. My skin never gives away my age.

Film ends with the close-up shot of the Santoor woman and her child.
Jingle: Santoor.. Santoor
Super: Making life more beautiful.

Santoor–Bangle Shop

Film opens on the Santoor woman going around looking at things at a fair.
Sound Effects: Music

Cut to the Santoor woman laughing.
Sound Effects: Music

Cut to close-up of Santoor soap.
Jingle: Filled with the goodness of turmeric and sandal.

Cut to old lady selling bangles.

Cut to a little girl emerging from one corner.
Girl: Mummy

Cut to ingredient shot of turmeric and sandal.
Jingle continues: ... Making life more beautiful.

The bangle seller putting bangles on the Santoor lady's hands.
Lady: On your wedding day I will make you wear 500 bangles.

Cut to Santoor woman laughing along with her kid.
Santoor woman speaking: It always happens. My skin never gives away my age.

Film ends with the close-up shot of the Santoor woman and her child.
Jingle: Santoor... Santoor
Super: Making life more beautiful.

Santoor–Aerobics

Film opens on aerobics session with the Santoor woman in a strenuous workout.
Sound Effects: Music

One of the girls runs to the Santoor woman.
The girl: Which college do you study in?

Cut to Santoor lady hugging the Kid.
The girl: You cannot judge her age by looks of her skin.

Close-up of other girls in the aerobics session. One of the girls (commenting about the Santoor woman): How beautiful.
I've never seen her here before.

Santoor woman laughs at the comments of the girl.
Santoor Woman: College? Me?

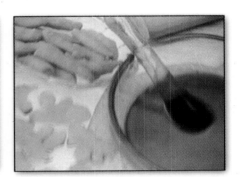

Cut to ingredient shot of turmeric and sandal.
Jingle: Filled with the goodness of turmeric and sandal.

Cut to close-up of the Santoor woman.
Sound Effects: Music

Cut to one little girl emerging from one corner.
Girl: Mummy

Film ends with the close-up shot of the Santoor soap.
Jingle: Making life more beautiful. Santoor...Santoor.

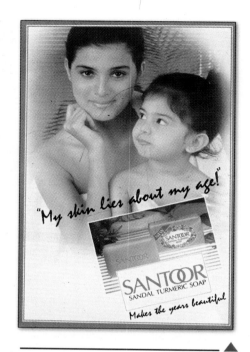

Poster
Santoor Soap
"My skin lies about my age..."

Poster
Santoor Soap
"Makes my life beautiful."

Press Ad
Santoor Soap
"The secret of younger looking skin..."

executing the younger looking skin promise was by using a 'mistaken identity' route. While Indian women felt they should look young and receive compliments form others, the best representation was when a married woman with a child (the ultimate proof of womanhood!) gets mistaken for a younger woman–by a group of women!

BINGO!

The first film that went on the floors had a group of college girls accosting our Santoor woman in a bookshop, asking her in which college she studies ... only to be surprised when her daughter runs up screaming 'Mummy'!

The first film was tested and scored amazingly well in the simulated test market (STM).

Santoor was on a roll. The format of 'mistaken identity' soon got extended into a number of situations:

- Bookshop
- Wedding
- Bangle shop
- Aerobics

Over the next nine years, the brand had undergone three facelifts, packaging changes, fragrance improvements etc. Its advertising had remained very much rooted on the discovery made in 1989 !

RESULTS

Santoor has not looked back since 1989. Against the time limit of 2 years, Santoor achieved its targeted volume of 5000 TPA in only 18 months. The brand sales have consistently been higher than that of the market and Santoor is one of the leading brands of soap in several large states.

If one were to view this achievement in the light of several market realities, the magnitude of the achievement becomes more gigantic:

- TOMCO has been bought over by Hindustan Lever
- Swastik has virtually disappeared
- Godrej brands were bought over by Procter & Gamble, only to be sold back
- Procter & Gamble's foray into the Indian soap market has met with failure.

In the light of all this, Wipro, with its focussed efforts and advertising that worked in the market, was able to build a brand and create enduring brand value.

This is an ultimate proof of the fact that good advertising works to build sales in the short term and build brand value over time.

Santoor: Brand Building Tips

In a highly competitive market with numerous brands, it is necessary to look beyond mere product ingredients, Santoor's success was a result of moving from ingredients (sandal and turmeric) to benefits (beautiful skin–younger looking skin). Further the brand's advertising could deliver the promise (younger looking skin), through a creative device (mistaken identity), whereby building a brand and a large volume of brand loyal consumers.

SUNDROP: Positioning for Healthy Success

BACKGROUND

In the mid-1980s, when ITC decided to expand beyond its tobacco business, it chose to enter the edible oil business. The edible oil market was growing rapidly, with demand far outstripping supply, making India a net importer of oils and oilseeds. This prompted the government to treat oils/oilseeds as a national priority and to set up the oilseeds technology mission.

The business potential was vast, offering excellent growth opportunities and made sound commercial sense. More importantly, ITC had the requisite agri-based skills and enjoyed the trust of farmers due to its long standing relationship with the community through its Leaf Tobacco Division.

THE COOKING MEDIUM MARKET

The cooking medium market in India is broken into three major segments: Filtered oils, Refined oils and *Vanaspati* (hydrogenated fats). *Ghee*, which used to be the main cooking medium, gave way to *Vanaspati* and other oils because of its high cost and implications. The market was characterised by vast variations in the types of oil used due to regional user preferences. Groundnut oil was used extensively in the west and south, mustard oil in the east and north, coconut and sesame/*til* in Kerala and Tamil Nadu. The market was also characterised by multiple usage of oils for cooking different types of dishes. For instance, while *Vanaspati* was used for everyday dishes, groundnut oil was used for speciality dishes in the west. A similar scenario existed in other regions as well. This resulted in the availability of a wide range of oils and oil brands in different price bands across the country.

The cooking medium market, in 1988 was estimated at 5.7 million tonnes, with edible oils accounting for 4.8 million tonnes (valued at Rs 140,000 million approximately). Of this, the unrefined oil segment accounted for 39 L (81 per cent) tonnes and was dominated primarily by groundnut, mustard and coconut oil. The consumption of refined oils was confined largely to urban areas, most of which was sold loose. The branded refined oil segment accounted for only 41,000 tonnes per annum.

Market Pyramid

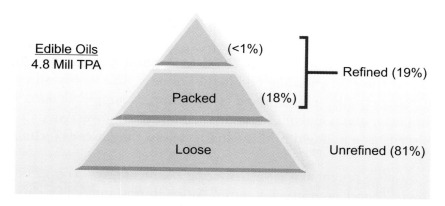

An analysis of the edible oil market threw up some interesting facts. The findings indicated that over the past few years, there was a shift from unrefined oils to refined oils due to increasing affluence, purity of the oil and an increasing awareness of health. Simultaneously, there was another ongoing shift from 'traditional' oils to 'new' oils like Sunflower, Safflower, Soya, etc. as they were perceived to be healthier. The study indicated that the refined oil segment was growing faster than the total edible oil market. It was expected that while the share of 'new' oils would continue to grow, traditional oils would continue to account for a major chunk.

Around 1988, the main offerings in packed refined oils were groundnut, sesame (*Til*), safflower (*Kardi*) and in a small way, sunflower oil and mustard oil. Groundnut oil accounted for 78 per cent of all refined oils with sunflower (2.7 per cent), safflower (23 per cent) and others accounting for the remainder.

The main brands in the refined edible oil segment were Postman (refined groundnut oil) with a 20 per cent share and Dalda refined groundnut oil with a 19 per cent share. Sunola (Tamil Nadu Agro Mills) and Flora (Lipton) were the only major refined sunflower oil brands with shares of 2.2 per cent and 0.2 per cent respectively.

Marketing Objectives

ITC Agrotech's objective was very clear–to obtain leadership in the edible refined oil segment. It had identified the 'new' refined oils segment as offering the maximum potential for growth. This called for providing the consumer with a superior quality product at competitive prices available in different pack sizes for expanding the market.

The company had decided on sunflower oil for several reasons. It was perceived to be a 'healthy' oil, could be grown in semi-arid areas as it was a hardy crop, gave 3–4 crops a year as against groundnut that gives only one, and important enough, could be priced very competitively vis-à-vis refined groundnut oil. The objectives for the brand were clear–achieve volume objectives, set up the distribution network and build a dealer franchise and equity with the customer.

The company had invested substantially in the manufacturing infrastructure to ensure that the oil was of the best quality–clear, low on colour and odourless. The distribution network was set up with care. Outlets were selected on the basis of this stock turnover potential. New and non-conventional outlets were approached like general stores and chemists. Service levels were pre-determined for each outlet.

What's in a Name?—Branding

The name 'Sundrop' was chosen after extensive research. The brand cued the category at the product level, and at another level associated the brand with 'goodness'/'purity' in every drop.

Understanding the Consumer

Before launching the brand, it was essential to understand the consumer and gauge her needs, identify different segments and the target group for the brand.

It was found that after milk, oil accounted for the highest cash outlay in a housewife's monthly expenses. Also, due to bulk purchases which led to higher cash disbursals at one go, she was highly price –sensitive when it came to edible oil purchase. Brand loyalty–except for Postman which had a captive loyal segment–was very low.

Research also indicated that the key attributes sought by the consumer in an edible oil were taste, quality (purity, colour, odour), health and value for money.

WHO USES WHAT

The National Council of Applied Economic Research (NCAER) has done seminal work on the usage of consumer products across urban and rural India. These studies are being repeated at periodic intervals giving marketeers a wealth of information.

India is a country with over 160 million households. Who buys what kind of products ?

As can be expected, the most widely used products are washing cakes and toilet soaps. Thanks to the Nirma revolution, washing powders are not far behind. But if we were to look at shampoos, face creams and nail enamels, the numbers shrink. But these were figures pertaining to 1994-95. The numbers for 1999-2000 should, hopefully, look a little better.

Upto 10 Million	Nail Enamel Lipstick etc.
11 to 30 Million	Shampoos/ Face Creams etc.
31-60 Million	Packaged Biscuits etc.
61-90 Million	Telcom Powder, Bulbs etc.
Over 90 Million Households	Washing Cake, Tea etc.

What does this imply? For certain product categories, the route to growth is market expansion. Witness the spurt of activity in the shampoo market. For certain product categories that are highly penetrated like washing powders/cakes, the route is for getting consumers to upgrade or graduate. Witness the activity level in detergents with newer and newer product offerings.

Source: Business Today
February 22–March 6, 1996

Cooking Oil Consumer Wish List

Tangible Promises	Intangible Promises
- Taste Enhancement	- Healthy Family
- Purity	- Love and Affection
- Colour	- Caring Mother
- Odour	- Great Cook
- Value for Money	

Filtered oil consumption, being largely an urban phenomenon, was primarily seen in the middle and upper middle income households. The housewife was value-and economy-conscious and was concer-ned about the health and well-being of her family.

Based on this, the target consumer was defined as a modern, aware, educated housewife in the 21 to 44 years age group using refined branded oils, primarily groundnut oil, who was concerned about the well-being and health of her family.

> *They said so*
>
> "....in an economy that is striving to break the age-old bondage of man to misery, want and destitution, marketing is also the catalyst for the transmutation of latent resources into actual resources, of desires into accomplishments, and the development of responsible economic leaders and informed economic citizens."
>
> • **Peter F. Drucker,**
> "Marketing and Economic Development"
> *Journal of Marketing* (January 1958)

Positioning Sundrop—Competitive Scan

The advertising for competitive brands was examined to evaluate and identify a positioning platform for the brand. Most of the brands were positioned on 'taste' and offered little or no health benefits. They all talked of taste and appreciation of tasty cooking by the whole family sitting around the dining table and had close-up shots of food being cooked.

The 'new' oils like safflower and sunflower were seen as healthy and all brands in this category were anchored around health in terms of 'reducing cholesterol' (Saffola), 'light and easy to digest' (Flora).

Options before Sundrop

Sundrop had three options to choose from: taste, price and health. Taste was ruled out as it was not unique, since everybody talked about it. However, since taste was a critical factor in brand choice, it was felt that it should be used as a supporting claim.

Despite Sundrop being cheaper than refined groundnut oil (RGO), price was not seen as a tenable long term benefit as all other refined sunflower oils (RSO) would be priced similarly.

Research had indicated the growing awareness and concern for 'health' and appreciation of oils, that had 'health' offers.

Of all the three options, the 'health' platform seemed to be the most enduring and effective. Saffola, for instance, had used the 'health' plank effectively with the 'reduces cholesterol' story involving testimonials from doctors. It had been able to create a strong franchise among consumers having heart, blood pressure and other health problems. Saffola's strength turned out to be a weakness as it had a very limited appeal outside its user base and led to negative perceptions regarding its taste. This led to 'Saffola' being used for the 'patient' and another oil brand for the rest of the family.

It was believed that the 'health' factor was more universal than the narrow confines as defined by Saffola. Research indicated that 'health':

- Could also mean maintenance of good health,
- Was applicable to all members of the family,
- Was characterised by lively energetic people.

This was supported by the increasing number of people involved in healthy activities like workouts, jogging etc. Furthermore, there was a large segment of people who did not have any health problems, but in view of the fast pace of life, were concerned about the long term prospects of their health.

Query Line

Q. A new brand has achieved in a market, 80% awareness, 20% trial and 2% repeat purchase. What would you recommend ?
- Increase advertising
- Do heavy sampling
- Change advertising
- Examine product quality
- All the above

Ans. *With 80% awareness, advertising has done one part of its job very well, i.e. to create awareness. One out of four aware consumers has tried the product, that may not be a bad number, depending on the brand's pricing, distribution etc. However only 1 in 10 consumers repeats the brand. So is the biggest problem something to do with consumers not being satisfied with the product quality or its price-value offering ?*

The best bet would be to examine product quality before spending any more money on advertising or venturing into new areas like sampling.

Based on this, Sundrop was positioned as the **'Healthy Oil for Healthy People'** (which to date serves as the sign-off line for all its advertising).

Creative Strategy and Execution

The creative task was twofold:

1. Position Sundrop as the healthy oil for healthy people
2. Ensure that this did not in any way erode the delivery of the 'taste' benefit.

In addition, it also had to ensure that it was perceptually as far away as possible from Saffola. It had to have a young, modern and premium feel without cueing "expensive". Last but not the least, it had to develop an execution that was relevant, distinctive and original so that it stood out of the clutter of ordinary food and oil advertising.

The creative execution, therefore, avoided the cliched, standard pictures of the family at the dinner table appreciating the food, food being cooked and the pack shot at the end of the advertisement.

The commercial instead featured a frisky, lively and energetic kid, a symbol of good health, who picks up the aroma of his mother's cooking, jumps out of bed and goes through his fantasy of larger than life mouth watering dishes. The use of the yellow colour in the settings was used to further reinforce the associations of health and cue the oil type. Another interesting device was the pouring of the oil that forms to become the Sundrop logo.

RESULTS

Within six months of its launch, Sundrop became the largest selling refined Sunflower oil, achieving a tonnage of 700 TPM. In the process, Sundrop redefined the category and expanded the Sunflower oil segment from 2.71% of the market to 23%, within 6 months of its launch. Since then Sundrop has consistently featured among the top 3 brands in the country. The major brands did face a temporary setback in the early 1990's with the launch of Dhara which played singularly on price and managed to woo in many loose consumers. But soon enough, Sundrop came to its own and is today the single largest refined oil brand in the country accounting for over 15% of the branded refined oils market. In its wake the Sundrop movement had taken the sunflower oil share as a fraction of the total consumer pack

Heard-in-the-Agency

(Amusing exchanges between 'anxious' servicing and even more 'anxious' creative folks.)

"But what if nobody reads beyond the headline."

ITC–Sundrop Sunflower Oil

Film opens with a boy smelling aroma of food.
SFX: Jingle starts.

Fantasy food shots begin.
Sound Effects: Music

Now the boy pushes open the door and enters the kitchen.
Sound Effects: Jingle continues

Cut to a 'puri' being cooked.
SFX: Jingle: ... Sundrop Super Refined Sunflower Oil

Boy cartwheeling near larger than life food.
Jingle: Sundrop Super Refined Sunflower Oil

Cut to mother hugging the kid.
Sound Effects: Jingle continues

Cut to boy jumping out of his bed and running towards the kitchen.
Sound Effects: Jingle... Healthy oil for healthy people

Cut to boy standing near larger than life puris.
Jingle: Healthy oil for healthy people

Film ends with close-up of the brand name.
Jingle: Sundrop Super Refined Sunflower Oil.
Healthy oil for healthy people.

BRAND BUILDING ADVERTISING ■

Press Ad
Sundrop Sunflower Oil
"Introducing the healthy oil for healthy people..."

Press Ad
Sundrop Sunflower Oil
"What makes Sundrop the healthy oil for healthy people..."

refined oil market from a mere 2.7% in June 1990 to a whopping 42% in 1997 to make it the largest species, mustard being a distant second at 22%. It is in order to conclude by saying that the film has been so effective in making the brand the market leader that it is still being continued as the main theme film, 10 years after the brand was launched.

> ## Sundrop: Brand Building Tips
>
> In a commodity market like cooking oils, there is an opportunity for a new brand to usurp the most important benefit offered by the key ingredient (Sundrop - Sunflower). Sundrop could leverage this into a very broad offering of 'Health and taste'. This broad offering, with evocative advertising not only built the brand but in fact propelled the entire category.

AMUL MALAI PANEER: Unforgettable Taste

Amul—a brand that is undoubtedly the number one food brand in the country, with total sales in excess of Rs 15 billion, with products that range from liquid milk to ice cream, from butter to *ghee* to cheese.

How can one keep the brand growing?

GCMMF (Gujarat Co-operative Milk Marketing Federation), the largest co-operative network in the country and marketeers of the Amul brand of products are constantly faced with this question.

Having been a part of Operation Flood that converted India from a milk deficit to a milk surplus country, their challenge is to keep the process going. But milk is a perishable commodity and a constant search is on for products that can be made out of milk.

This search led to the launch of a whole gamut of milk products:

- Butter
- *Ghee*
- Cheese
- Milk Powder
- Condensed Milk
- Chocolate
- Ice cream

Can there be more products that could be marketed under the Amul brand?

PANEER PASSION

Paneer is 'the cheese of India'!

Paneer is made in many north Indian homes (which have traditionally enjoyed surplus milk) and finds usage across a whole gamut of food preparations.

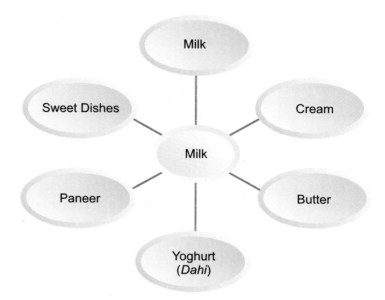

Paneer gets included in a whole gamut of dishes, both vegetarian and non-vegetarian. It also gets used as a cocktail snack!

Paneer was traditionally a homemade product. But with growing urbanisation and increasing time pressures on the Indian housewife, a market was emerging for ready-made *paneer*!

The first to capitalise on this trend was the unorganised dairy farm sector. Almost all 'dairy farms' and sweetmeat' shops started offering *paneer*. The quality and taste of *paneer* was dependent, among other things, on how 'fresh' it was. In this regard, the small unorganised sector scored a big plus. Given the size and scale of their operations, they could offer 'today's *paneer*' today!

The *paneer* market was developing rapidly, especially in the northern and western parts of the country.

The organised sector was slowly coming in, with Aarey and Gokul making tentative forays in the west.

GCMMF Paneer Plans

GCMMF tried its hand at Paneer marketing by testing a brand called Sugam, in Baroda in the mid 1990s. The product was refined, fine-tuned and ready for a large scale roll out.

The real challenge was to overcome the 'freshness' barrier. Could Amul tackle doubts about its freshness? Freshness matters so much to the consumer that she is willing to go an extra mile, to her regular *paneer* shop for getting real fresh *paneer*! Amul had already set up a cold chain to handle its ice cream marketing. It was felt that this cold chain would help deliver 'freshness' to the discerning consumer.

But it was felt that the brand had to be perceived differently from the neighbourhood *paneerwala*!

Amul Malai Paneer

It started with the name. Amul *paneer* was not just paneer but was '*malai paneer*' connoting:

- the vital quality of *paneer* as its ingredient
- made from rich cream
- a grainy texture that absorbs better (and is not rubbery)

The packaging was technologically designed to 'seal in' the freshness of *paneer*. The pack graphics portrayed an appetising shot of a *paneer* dish, "*paneer* peas *masala*". The pack's shelf (or freezer) appeal was aimed at giving it a premium feel!

Communication for Amul Malai Paneer

The communication task for Amul *malai paneer* was to drive home the point about it being soft, rich, creamy!

It was felt that the basic benefits of a branded packaged product, like those of hygiene, weight, price, will be obvious to the consumer. The communication, therefore, had to work on selling the 'taste' of the product, more than anything else.

WHO USES WHICH DURABLE

The National Council of Applied Economic Research (NCAER) has done seminal work on the penetration levels of various durables across urban and rural India. The study, conducted in 1993-94, gives an interesting snapshot.

Of the over 160 million Indian households, how many have which durables?

Mechanical Wrist Watches	127.4
Bicycles	77.8
Portable Radios	63.6
Ceiling Fans	49.6
B&W TVs	29.6
Colour TVs	9.9
Refrigerators	10.9
Washing Machines	3.6
Scooters	8.1

At the outset the Indian market looks vast, given the reasonably low level of penetration of most products. But if one were to superimpose the income earning potential of Indian households, one would exclude at least 83 million households, who are living at very low levels of income. This would imply that the real market for durables is the balance 80 million homes so where does that leave products that are already at this mark?

The answer, as TV marketeers have found, is to accelerate the replacement cycle whereby the upper classes upgrade while the lower classes get a 'reconditioned' TV at a very attractive price. That drives a number of durables, which are in reality unaffordable, into a large number of lower income homes.

At the other end is to get the upper classes to own more than one item, whether it be watches or music systems or fans. This increases purchases from already 'penetrated' upper classes.

Source: Business Today
February 22–March 6, 1996

Poster
Amul *Malai Paneer*
"Creamier. Tastier"

The 'taste' had to be sold without going against any established beliefs that might exist in the consumers' minds. This, it was felt, would be best achieved through the use of humour.

The Amul *paneer* TV commercial was centred around the great taste of *paneer* (visually seen in softness and richness) which is so good that it even helps an amnesia patient recover his lost memory!

The TV commercial was supported by limited press advertising during the launch phase. Amul *malai paneer*, as per Amul corporate values, was also priced attractively!

Post-launch researches have shown that the brand has gained high trials. The TV commercial has been well remembered and liked.

With Amul *malai paneer*, GCMMF has managed to open up yet another large opportunity for the Amul brand to take its message into more homes: The Taste of India Rules!

Heard-in-the-Agency
(Amusing exchanges between 'anxious' servicing and even more 'anxious' creative folks.)

" It's great copy ... but in

industrial advertising

people don't talk that way.

They don't talk the way

you and I do."

Amul *Malai Paneer*

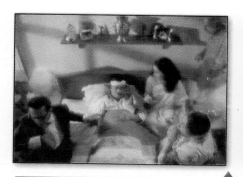

Film opens on a family gathered around the bed of a man, who has lost his memory.
Man: "Where am I"?

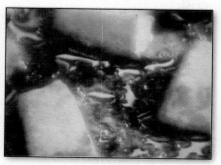

Cut to Amul 'Malai Paneer' being cooked.
MVO: "Creamy, soft, delicious—Amul 'Malai Paneer'.

Out of excitement he jumps out from his bed and hits a shelf above and knocks down the vase, which hits his head and his memory falters again: "Where am I now".

Cut to a doctor standing near the man.
Doctor: "Can you remind him of something from his past life, which will help him regain his memory"?

Cut to wife feeding her husband a dish made of Amul 'Malai Paneer'.
Sound Effects: Music

Cut to his wife and mother laughing at what has just happened to him again.

Close-up of man's wife who hits upon the idea of Amul 'Malai Paneer'.

The man gets back his memory and calls out the names of people in the household:
"Seema, Mamma, Pappa, Kakka..."

The film ends with a pack shot of Amul 'Malai Paneer'.

Amul *Malai Paneer*: Brand Building Tips

Ethnic foods can successfully leverage the emotional links of 'home-mother-wife' while offering the key benefits of 'taste' and 'ease of use'. Amul *malai paneer* advertising used humour in a 'home' setting to deliver its 'home taste' offer successfully.

CASE STUDY

CAPTAIN COOK ATTA: Branding a Commodity

BACKGROUND

A few years ago, the idea of a housewife buying a branded commodity like wheat flour (*atta*) would have been inconceivable. By and large, most commodity kitchen purchases were unbranded and bought in bulk from the local grocer. True, there were branded refined oils, basic spices and the like. But then, the idea of buying, say, branded *atta* or rice would have met with resistance from even upwardly mobile households. For them, good quality *atta* did not come from a bag, the quality of its contents which were unknown being, priced higher than wheat purchased from the grocer. It meant buying wheat of a particular quality, cleaning it and getting it ground at the neighbourhood flour mill (*chakkiwala*). In fact, the neighbourhood *chakkiwala* had become a tradition. Generations of mothers had been buying wheat grains and getting them ground at this institution.

This involved quite a bit of effort and inconvenience. But mother knew best and she certainly would not compromise on matters regarding the well-being and health of her family.

Upper Income Indian Housewife's Grocery Shopping Bag

Commodities	Brands
Rice	Tea
Sugar	Salt
Wheat/*Atta*	Coffee
Fruits	Oil(?)
Milk(?)	Butter
Spices	Biscuits
Vegetables	Milkfood
Pulses	Drinks
	Pickles(?)
	Ghee (?)
	Jams
	Spices(?)
	Bread

THE MARKET

Wheat, alongwith rice, forms the staple diet of the country. Of the total annual production of 55 mm tpa, most of it is grown and consumed in the north and west. As with rice, wheat is available in different grades sold at prices ranging between Rs 5/kg to Rs 14/kg, the best being 'MP Saharee' and 'Punjabi PC'.

Wheat is processed to produce other wheat-based products like '*maida*', '*sooji*', 'wheat flour' and 'wheat bran' for edible consumption and industrial use. The demand for 'wheat flour', '*maida*' and '*sooji*' emanates from the 'household' and the 'bakery / hotel' segments. The consumption of wheat has been growing rapidly due to increase in population size, urbanisation and increasing income levels.

INFOLINE

MEDIA HABITS OF INDIA

The National Readership Survey VI, done in 1997 and Indian Readership Study, 1998, capture the media habits of urban and rural India.

IRS 98 lists the total number of households, urban plus rural at 173.8 million, with 47.3 million urban households.

Press medium reaches 59 percent of urban adults and 27 per cent of rural adults. Television reaches 76 percent of urban homes and 33 per cent of rural homes.

According to the NRS VI, 1997, there are 48.6 million urban households. This translates into 171 million adults (15 years +) living in urban India (on an average 3.5 adults per household). In urban India, the reach of various media are as follows :

Press	59%
TV	78%
Radio	29%
Cinema	38%

Media like radio and cinema are giving way to television. In fact, in urban India 69 per cent of all households own a TV and an amazing 31 per cent have a cable–satellite connection.

Source: A&M, May 1-15, 1998

Responservice February, 1998

Of all the wheat-based products, consumption of wheat flour is the highest accounting for as much as 60–70 per cent of total wheat production. Traditionally, wheat was purchased from the local grocer, cleaned and then ground either at home or at the neighbourhood flour mill. Depending upon the size of the household, the consumption of wheat flour ranged between 2 kg–5 kg among light users to 15–20 kg per month among heavy users. Since wheat flour was a staple food, wheat was often purchased in bulk and stored at home, especially in the north and in Gujarat. As and when the need arose, the wheat grain was ground either at home or at the flour mill, to ensure freshness of the wheat flour.

Although wheat was normally purchased and ground, the concept of packed/branded *atta* was not exactly new. There was a small segment of users buying either packed *atta* from the flour mill or branded *atta* offered by players like Trupthi, Shakti Bhog and Green World, especially in the north.

Market trends indicated a definite shift from loose to branded products across various product categories and pointed towards a potential in branded goods, so long as it offered the consumer quality and convenience.

They Said So

"If.....you want to apply positioning thinking to your own company's situation, here are some questions to ask yourself:
1. *What position, if any, do we already own in the prospect's mind?*
2. *What position do we want to own?*
3. *What companies must be out-gunned if we are to establish that position?*
4. *Do we have enough marketing money to occupy and hold the position?*
5. *Do we have the guts to stick with one consistent positioning concept?*
6. *Does our creative approach match our positioning strategy?"*

• **Jack Trout and Al Ries**,
"Positioning cuts through chaos in Market place"
Advertising Age (May 1, 1972)

CAPTAIN COOK

The first taste of success came for Captain Cook, with its attempt to enter the salt category via the branded commodity route. The brand was a winner, carving a significant market share for itself and giving Tata Salt, the leader in the category, a run for its money.

The success of Captain Cook Salt indicated changing consumer preferences and demonstrated the vast potential in the commodity market that could be tapped, provided it was done effectively.

On the basis of this, it was decided to enter the commodity market in a big way. Entry in the commodity market was governed by several criteria that were laid down. The market had to be large and growing, in volume and value terms, and it had to be a high involvement product offering scope for value addition in manufacturing/processing so as to command a loyalty for the quality and convenience offered.

Several commodities were evaluated before wheat flour was decided upon. It met all the criteria laid down and the company believed it had the necessary expertise to market branded wheat flour. Its distribution network was already in place and its brand, Captain Cook, enjoyed a strong standing among the trade and consumers.

In 1993, FCB-Ulka was appointed as the advertising agency and entrusted with the task of launching the product and building a brand out of it.

When FCB-Ulka was given the assignment, it initiated research to identify consumer perceptions of *atta*, the possible need gaps in the overall market and consumer perceptions of branded *atta*.

The findings indicated three consumer segments based on the preparation of *atta*: those who ground the wheat at home those getting it ground at the flour mill and those already buying packed/branded *atta*. The findings identified the second segment as being the biggest and possibly most amenable to change.

The purchase, storage and usage patterns indicated that the effort and inconvenience of purchasing the wheat, cleaning it and getting it ground at the mill was offset by the consumer's feeling of control over the quality of the *atta* and the satisfaction of doing the best for her family.

The housewife, however, faced a few problems with the flour ground at the mill, such as adulteration of the flour by the miller, impurities and dirt getting into the *atta* and less quantity of *atta* returned to her due to process loss. This, however, was preferable to a packed or branded *atta* because none of the existing offerings allayed her fears and apprehensions regarding the quality of the *atta*, freshness and the hygiene/cleanliness factor.

Atta Alternatives

	Miller Route	Branded Route
Advantages	• Control on grain • Fresh atta • Price–value	• Guaranteed quantity • Convenience
Disadvantages	• Adulteration • Cheating • Inconvenience	• Quality of grain suspect • Old stocks • Price–value

Our recipe for a *phuli hui puri* calls for a better atta.

Rediscover the joy of cooking

Press Ad
Captain Cook *Atta*
"Our recipe for a *phuli hui puri...*"

Query Line

Q. Our brand's biggest competitor has just launched a big consumer promotion (free gift) campaign. Our response should be:

- Wait and watch
- Launch a bigger promotion campaign
- Increase advertising
- Launch a consumer contest
- None of the above

Ans. *Consumer promotion campaigns usually have a good short term effect. But their effectiveness in building long term brand equity is unproven. It will not be wise to launch yet another promotion campaign while the competitor, is running one. It would, draw attention to the competitors campaign. Wait and watch is not a proactive option. The best choice would be to increase advertising and take other brand support measures in the market.*

Consumer Profile

On the basis of this, the consumer profile was defined as a housewife, 25 years+, in A1/A2, B1/B2 SECs with the capacity to spend fairly high levels of the monthly income on things important to her family. Although she felt that conventional practices provided the best quality, she was open to other alternatives, but needed the reassurance to switch to a modern method and product.

Positioning

Research had indicated that the target consumers' key apprehensions revolved around the quality of the grain, adulteration, hygiene, taste and the freshness of the wheat flour. It revealed that if these aspects were considerably reinforced, she would be satisfied at both the rational and emotional levels by making her feel that she was doing the best for her family.

She had to be given the feeling that by using the product, she would not have to relinquish her control, but could place her trust in the product that would take care of her family's well-being just the way she would.

The product was hence positioned as *"made from the finest quality wheat, to give you tasty rotis which you can enjoy with your family"*.

The Advertising

As the advertising had to encounter a barrage of negative perceptions, which had to be converted into positives, the advertising task was defined as creating a premium image for Captain Cook *Atta* and establishing it as a product made from the best quality ingredients vis-à-vis both branded and loose *atta*.

To build credibility, enhance appeal and make the advertising memorable, the advertising used subtle humour in a family situation around an 'expert', a farmer. The creative translation of the positioning statement was '*sone jaise gehun se bana*' (made from wheat as good as gold).

The advertising, therefore, focused on the richness of the wheat used to convey good quality and featured an upmarket farmer, coming home to a dinner comprising *rotis* made from Captain Cook, complaining to nobody in particular about the quality control in the Captain Cook *Atta* factory while finishing off *roti* after *roti*, at which point the wife interrupts his diatribe, explaining that all the *rotis* that he was endlessly consuming were made from Captain Cook *Atta*. The farmer loses his composure for a moment, but regains it and asks for yet another *roti*.

The housewife and her little daughter have the last laugh!

The Launch

Captain Cook *Atta* was launched in Bombay in June 1994 in 2 kg packs priced at Rs 21 following the test marketing in Pune earlier. Soon it rolled out to the rest of Maharashtra, Hyderabad, Bangalore, Ahmedabad and Delhi. By mid-1995, the brand was available across the country.

Heard-in-the-Agency

(Amusing exchanges between 'anxious' servicing and even more 'anxious' creative folks.)

"A focus group up north proved conclusively

that women between the ages of 7 and 93

object to the words

NEW, *Improved*, INTRODUCING, AT LAST!

As a writer surely you can offer a substitute.

Can we afford to offend all women?"

The Campaign and the Response

The campaign comprised a 60 second TV film, radio spots, press advertisements, POP and outdoor publicity.

During the initial months, the sales surpassed all expectations leaving retailers in a squeeze for stocks. The advertising succeeded enormously in drawing consumers to Captain Cook, moving away from their age-old habits of using the local miller.

Captain Cook proved beyond doubt that Indian housewives are willing to move out of the 'commodity' mindset given, the right incentives—a strong brand promise, a good value proposition and an imagery that proves to her that she is the 'master of all she surveys'!

Poster
Captain Cook *Atta*
"Made out of golden wheat..."

Captain Cook: Brand Building Tips

Converting consumers from 'unbranded' 'commodities' to brands is one of the biggest challenges facing marketeers in India. Captain Cook achieved the breakthrough by showing what was behind the brand (ingredient : golden wheat). The brand presented the product story through an interesting storyline-based film that entertained while educating the consumer.

Captain Cook *Atta*–Farmer

Film opens on an angry young farmer who comes home for lunch.
Farmer: "Those Captain Cook 'Atta' people are really troubling us farmers."

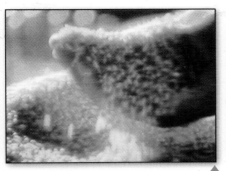

Cut to wheat being taken in a hand and farmer continues to speak: "They want every grain to be of the same shape and size."

Cut to amazed looking farmer.
Farmer: "You also use Captain Cook 'Atta'?"

Cut to shot of 'roti' being made

Close-up of wheat grains and farmer still continues speaking.
".... And should be golden in colour. As if they are making gold."

Captain Cook 'Atta' is unveiled.

Farmer continues speaking:
"Selling wheat to them is a big hassle."

Cut to farmer's wife and kid laughing at his comments.
Wife: "Because they are so particular about quality of the wheat, their 'atta' will also be good. And you are eating so many 'rotis!'"

Film ends with close-up of Captain Cook Atta
Super and Voice-Over (VO):
"Captain Cook 'Atta'.
Made from golden wheat."

SECTION

Brand Building Consumer Durables Advertising

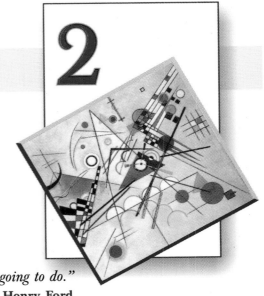

2

"You can't build a reputation on what you are going to do."
• **Henry Ford**

*"You can have brilliant ideas, but if you can't get them across,
your ideas won't get you anywhere."*
• **Lee Iacocca**

S ony. The brand that spells innovation, quality, reliability. Across the world Sony is probably the most recognised consumer durable brand. Obviously the Sony brand was built through constant innovation and consistent brand building communication. Today "It's a Sony" at the end of the television commercial says it all.

CONSUMER DURABLES

How does one define a consumer durable? How is it different from a consumer product FMCG?

- In price?
- In longevity?
- In involvement?

Consumer products are bought by consumers at regular intervals. For cigarettes the purchase is made daily. For soaps, it is probably monthly, and so on. As a result, every time the consumer goes to make her purchases, she can change the brand. In effect, brand loyalty is under test every day, every week, every month. No doubt, because of this constant choice opportunity, the maximum amount of 'brand' studies have been done in the area of consumer products.

Unlike consumer products, consumer durables, by definition, are not bought at short periodic intervals. Often the replacement cycle can run into years. In the case of some products, like cars, it could even be a decade. Given this long lock-in period, the role of a 'brand' becomes somewhat different. Further, the value of purchase is often counted in terms of the number of months, salary spent on it. All this leads to making the consumer decision-making process a long, detailed and time-consuming one.

So if we were to go back to our first equation of: Brand = Product + Image, in the case of consumer durables, the equation may be as follows:

$$\text{Brand} = \text{Product} + \text{Image}$$

How Does Advertising Work

In the FCB grid examined earlier, consumer durables would fit into the High Involvement–Think, or High Involvement–Feel quadrants.

By their nature consumer durables, TVs, refrigerators, washing machines, two wheelers, fans, etc. are all high value purchases. Every purchase is preceded by several mandatory processes—varying with the type of product and the socio-economic class of the consumer.

Consumer Check List

- Heard of the brand before? Used it before?
- Know anyone using it? What do they say?
- Where is it available? Where else?
- Which are the leading brands? Model options?
- What after-sales service is needed? Who offers the best?
- What features do we need? Any others?
- What financing options are available? Cash discount?
- What is the price? Any extras?
- What is the expected life? Resale value?
- Do I really need it now? Is it the right brand?
- Did I take the right decision? Any assurances?

Brand Building Advertising

Advertising with respect to consumer durables, has to play several roles from building awareness, to demonstrating the product, creating aspirational values, etc. In addition, advertising plays the role of reassuring consumers who have the brand, that they have made the right choice, and of reducing post-purchase dissonance.

Does this mean that all consumer durables advertising has to be packed with data and be very rational, very direct?

If we were to layer on top of the requirements of consumer durables advertising, with what is advertising, some answers emerge. Advertising by nature is intrusive in nature. So to be heard advertising has to:

- Sound and look unique
- Be relevant to the target consumer
- Be believable

Over and above all this, advertising has to be 'likeable'. Increased likeability increases brand recall and brand preference.

In addition, consumer durable purchases are long drawn out and the entire process could run into months. Advertising, during this process, is actively 'consumed' by the target public. But advertising needs to stand out from the clutter and keep the consumer hooked on to the brand right through the process.

After purchase, it is often the advertising both in media and through guarantees and direct mail that needs to keep the consumer happy with his purchase.

So, while it is true that in consumer durables a lot will depend on the features, price–value offering, after-sales service, a lot can be achieved through consistent brand building advertising.

Model for Consumer Durables Advertising

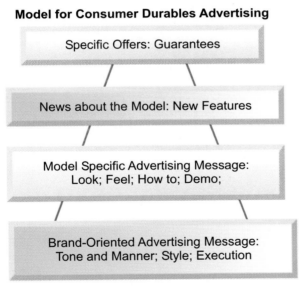

Most importantly, consumer durable advertising is often focused on specific features, new model offerings, new offers. If advertising, across various product/model offerings can stay tuned to the "brand", advertising budgets can work extra hard and brands can be built across products.

CASES

The following section consists of four cases covering a range of consumer durable brands. They include a new model launch, a turnaround case and two cases of enduring brands which have used advertising to build sales volume and brand equity over a period of time.

CASE STUDY

LML VESPA: Build Your Own Mountain

Throughout the early 1980s, Bajaj Auto had a stranglehold on the two-wheeler market. It had a waiting list that promised deliveries after six years or more. If a consumer wanted to buy a scooter, he had the option of buying the by then obsolete Lambretta, a second hand scooter, if he was lucky to get one cheap, or pay a premium of as much as Rs 4,000 to Rs 6,000 if he wanted a new Bajaj scooter. Alternatively, he could place his booking for a Bajaj and wait for its delivery.

In the early 1980s, the government relaxed restrictions on the automobile industry. This led to a spate of new entries in the two wheeler market. Although most of the activity was in the motorcycle segment, the scooter segment also saw a few players come in, the key players being Lohia Machines Limited in collaboration with Piaggio, Italy and Kinetic Engineering in association with Honda Motors, Japan. The other new scooter manufacturers were primarily state government undertakings of the likes of AP Scooters, Gujarat Motors, etc.

MARKET SCENARIO (1986-1990)

By 1986, the Indian scooter market grew to a size of 6,00,000. Bajaj Auto, by virtue of being the only large player, continued to retain its dominance in the market. Although Bajaj Auto had an installed capacity of 1,00,000 scooters per month, its actual production was far below that. With demand exceeding supply, the sales of Bajaj scooters were purely production-led. Quite expectedly, its scooters commanded large premiums. Faced with little choice, consumers willingly paid hefty sums as premiums for a new Bajaj scooter resulting in a thriving black market. This black marketeering in scooters only increased the 'perceived' value of a Bajaj scooter.

Soon after the government lifted restrictions on the automobile industry, Lohia Machines Limited had entered into a collaboration with Piaggio, Italy, of Vespa fame. Rather than import CKD/ SKD kits and assemble the scooters in India, LML Vespa set up a state-of-the-art plant with a production capacity of 20,000 scooters per month. In 1986, LML Vespa introduced the 100 cc 'NV' model. The design and styling were

A COUNTRY OF SHOPKEEPERS

India is known to be a country of shopkeepers, from time immemorial. A study conducted by the Asian Information Marketing and Social Research in 1996 puts the total number of retail outlets in urban India at an amazing 2.1 million! This implies one shop for every 125 urban residents! These are only shops stocking branded and packaged fast moving consumer goods (FMCG)!

Obviously most of these outlets, i.e. 64% are categorised as very small!

SHOP TYPE BY ZONE—URBAN

	All India	North	East	West	South
Grocers	32.4	34.7	32.0	32.2	30.2
Pan/Bidi	14.6	7.1	21.2	13.1	19.1
Food Shops	11.6	11.8	7.9	14.9	12.0
General Stores	10.1	12.4	9.1	12.0	6.6
Electrical/Hardware	6.7	8.3	5.6	7.6	5.7
Chemists	5.7	6.0	5.8	5.0	5.7
Cosmetic stores	3.7	3.9	3.6	3.2	3.9
Others	15.2	15.7	14.7	11.9	17.4
Total	100.0	100.0	100.0	100.0	100.0
Total Outlets	100.0	30.4	21.5	21.5	26.5
Total Population	100.0	26.2	18.8	26.8	28.2

As a category grocers number the most, across all regions, followed by *pan/bidi* shops. North and east zones have a higher density of retail outlets as compared to south and west zones.

It is obvious that no FMCG can achieve a 100% reach, even if it wants to. Lux, Lifebuoy and Colgate are present in over one million shops! A number of *pan/bidi* shops stock these as well!

The need of an FMCG brand is to achieve a critical level of distribution through an organised sales effort and let the wholesale trade carry the brand into the next tier of shops.

The use of the retail point of purchase as a brand communication medium is growing rapidly with the increased availability of display shelves in A class outlets. But given the variation in size and shape of space available, it is necessary to think of modular designs that can be adapted to fit into small spaces!

Source: 'Brand Equity', *The Economic Times*
March 5–11, 1997

contemporary and offered unique features like the spare tyre placed inside the body, indicators etc. The same year also saw the launch of the Kinetic Honda, a 100 cc scooter with automatic transmission. Although the response to the Kinetic Honda was lukewarm due to negative consumer perceptions, the 'NV' from LML Vespa was received with enthusiasm. Soon, LML Vespa had a waiting list of several years as well. The positive response to LML Vespa was, in part, due to the non-availability of Bajaj scooters and the novelty of the product in a market long since accustomed to only one product.

It seemed that Bajaj's philosophy was only one step ahead of that of Henry T Ford's: "The consumer can have the Ford in any colour as long as it's black". It offered the Bajaj in two basic models, the Chetak and the Super (the Bajaj Vespa having been discontinued in the early 1980s). For almost two decades, there had been no changes or upgradations in terms of design and styling.

By 1988, LML Vespa emerged as the second largest scooter manufacturer. However, it owed its success in part to the demand–supply gap caused by the non-availability of Bajaj rather than on the merit of its product performance or brand image. As a result, its sales fluctuated in direct proportion to Bajaj's sales, peaking when the latter's sales were down and dropping with the latters increasing availability.

> *"Confusion has set in. In many categories customers no longer perceive any large differences in products. Thus brand choice will not be based on a rational search of all brands in the category but on a brand that was previously tried. Or the leader. Or the one positioned to the prospect's segment."*
>
> **• Jack Trout and Al Ries,**
> *The Positioning Era: A View Ten Years Later Advertising Age* (July 16, 1979)

They Said So

By the end of the decade, however, LML's sales went into a steep decline. Clearly its effort to increase its market share with the introduction of Bajaj look-alike models had failed. Furthermore, the product was not without its share of problems. The consumer who was used to a 150 cc scooter, could not reconcile himself to the thought of a 100 cc scooter. At that point of time, the measure of a two-wheeler was a function of its cubic capacity and not its brake horsepower (BHP). Only later did it dawn on him that it was the BHP that mattered and not the cc. In the meantime, Kinetic Honda had overcome its initial teething problems and by meeting with increasing consumer acceptance, had begun closing the gap with LML.

With the decline in LML's sales showing no signs of abatement and cancellation of bookings on the rise, LML Vespa made a few product

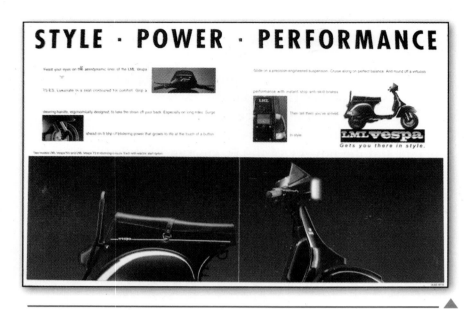

Press Ad
LML Limited
"Style. Power. Performance."

Query Line

Q. A sample of 100 men in Bombay can be used to predict the behaviour of the entire population of males in Bombay (tick one):

• Never, the sample is too small
• Definitely, the sample is enough
• It depends

Ans. *Contrary to popular belief, sample size has little to do with population size. (It would otherwise be impossible to do opinion polls.) Sample size depends on the expected 'p' or proportion value. So if we are sure that the sample is perfectly random, then a sample size of 100 may be enough to predict behaviour (all men in Bombay wear a shirt!). The best answer therefore is: It depends.*

modifications and upgraded it to 150 cc. The scooter was relaunched on the 'safety' platform and additional money pumped in for its promotion.

During the same period, Bajaj Auto stepped up the production of its scooters. The premiums which it had commanded earlier vanished, due to free availability. Almost as a direct consequence, LML's sales dropped like a lead-weighted stone and were down to an anaemic 5000 units a month—5 per cent of Bajaj's monthly sales and 25 per cent of its production capacity.

THE RESURRECTION

In this dismal scenario, FCB-Ulka Advertising was appointed to handle the promotion and advertising for LML Vespa.

The first thing that the agency did on being assigned the account, was an analysis of the scooter market to identify the key factors determining the brand choice. An analysis revealed that LML Vespa had fallen in the

Press Ad
LML Limited
"Great relationships begin here..."

classic trap facing all new entrants in a market dominated by a giant. Rather than write its own rules of the game, it had instead let Bajaj define them.

LML Vespa's advertising was effective in giving the product an image of safety. But safety was not a discriminator affecting brand choice, simply

Positioning of Two-Wheelers

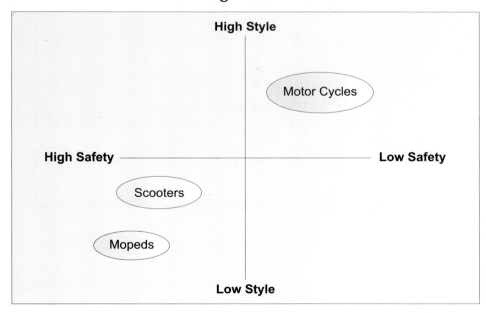

because Bajaj was not seen as an 'unsafe' scooter. Furthermore, despite the edge it enjoyed by way of Piaggio's superior technology and the latest designs, LML Vespa had not exploited this opportunity.

In the 1970s, Bajaj had entered into a tie-up with Piaggio to manufacture and market scooters under the Bajaj Vespa name. When Bajaj withdrew from the agreement in the early 1980s, the 'Vespa' heritage still belonged to Bajaj, in the consumers' mind—a misconception that LML had never tried to correct either by way of its product design and/or its advertising.

An analysis revealed that by virtue of it being the pioneer in scooters, Bajaj had placed over 5.5 million scooters on the road, building for itself an image of 'trust' along the way. The advertising for the brand also effectively reinforced this position.

It was clear that LML needed a product policy and positioning that clearly differentiated it from Bajaj. Although the product policy to design new models would take time, it was evident that if LML Vespa had to be saved from extinction, its advertising would have to start delivering immediately.

Press Ad
LML Limited
"Vespa Select, Take the joy of riding..."

Press Ad
LML Limited
"Vespa Select. Take the joy of riding..."

On the basis of these market findings, the agency realized that the key to success lay in avoiding any head-on competition with Bajaj. This could be achieved by positioning LML Vespa in such a way as to reposition Bajaj, while creating a distinct identity for the brand which could not be appropriated by Bajaj in the future.

Positioning

The next step was to develop the brand positioning for LML Vespa. To arrive at this, the agency undertook a study to identify consumer perceptions about Bajaj. Earlier research findings had indicated that Bajaj's strengths lay in its fuel efficiency, ease of maintenance, reliability, durability, its resale value and its reputation—all the key factors influencing brand choice. LML Vespa's strengths were seen as superior technology, driving comfort, safety, power and aesthetics.

The findings of the image study conducted among consumers revealed that Bajaj's success dictated its positioning. With more than five-and-a-half million Bajaj scooters on the road, Bajaj was seen as an average middle class person's scooter, meant for the family man. It was the functional, value-for-money (VFM) scooter. It, however, evoked strong positive, emotional associations among consumers best described by the term "the great indian spirit"—an emotion it successfully encashed upon with the '*hamara Bajaj*' campaign.

FCB-Ulka believed that Bajaj's down to earth image enabled LML Vespa to tap a different motivational vein, which would reposition Bajaj at the other end of the perceptual continuum. Accordingly, the brand was positioned around 'power and style' and the brand was given a distinct upmarket image.

The positioning of LML Vespa on the 'power and style' platform was unique in terms of the fact that traditionally scooters were not associated with power and style – this was a property normally owned by motor-cycles, which unlike scooters had a macho appeal. Both the agency and the client believed that the scooters' stereotyped image as "fuddy-duddy and old-fashioned" was a myth that would explode as newer models of scooters with improved aesthetics entered the market, and that the advantage would lie with the first player to exploit this opportunity.

The desired image for LML Vespa was defined as 'the aspirational middle class person's scooter, meant for the young person. It should be international product that offers superior performance and contemporary styling'.

TARGET PERSON

The Creative Strategy

The advertising campaign for the relaunch comprised a TV film, press campaign and point of

Bajaj	LML Vespa
Male 25 years + Middle Class Married "Conservative" "Family-oriented"	Male 25 years + Middle Class Married/Unmarried "Progressive" "Free-spirited"

sale (POS) items for display in dealer showrooms. Early on, it was decided to use TV as the main medium and for theme advertising, which would seek to create and reinforce the desired image and brand position. Press, on the other hand, was to be used as a support medium for theme advertising and for new product introductions.

The TV film, developed for the relaunch, featured a youth and a girl on an LML Vespa scooter with quick inter-cuts of the product, where the emphasis on its aesthetics and styling. The ambience was distinctly upmarket, youthful and trendy, in line with the premium imagery desired. The music score was accordingly set to a lively pop-rock beat.

Creative Brief

- *Single-Minded Proposition*
  LML Vespa is the more stylish scooter
- *Support for the Proposition*
  LML Vespa is made with contemporary Italian design and technology
  LML Vespa offers several product plusses (like side indicators, stepney—inside—body etc.
  LML Vespa is sleeker looking than any other scooter on the roads
  LML Vespa offers a powerful performance on the road

The press campaign comprised full page double spread colour advertisements with the product being the hero. The copy was kept to the bare minimum and the emphasis, as in the TV film, was on its contemporary looks and styling. The POS developed primarily comprised posters and were extensions of the press campaign and signed off with the base-line common to the TV film and press campaign—'Power, Style and Performance'.

The Media

Given the relatively limited budget as compared to Bajaj's mammoth ad spends, the agency decided to go in for a concentrated burst during the launch phase followed by a pulsing strategy to ensure visibility throughout the year.

The Response

The brand's advertising strategy paid off. The monthly sales rose from 5000 units to 16,000 units in a span of two years. The next burst of advertising further strengthened the imagery of LML Vespa as a great looking scooter and saw the brand's share rise. By 1996, a decade after

LML Vespa–Power

Film is a montage of stylised shots opening on a scooter.

Jingle: You've got the style

Jingle: You've got the power

Sound Effects: Music

Sound Effects: Music

Jingle: You've got the style

Jingle: You've got the power...

Sound Effects: Music

VO: Style. Power. Performance
LML Vespa

LML Vespa–Saxophone

Film opens on a man playing a saxophone.

Sound Effects: Music

Sound Effects: Music

Cut to shot of LML starting and moving on its own.
Sound Effects: Music

Sound Effects: Music

Sound Effects: Music

Cut to man playing a saxophone.

Sound Effects: Music

The film ends with the man appreciating the scooter.
VO: Style. Power. Performance
LML VESPA

LML Vespa–Cello

Film opens on a man playing a cello.

Sound Effects: Music

Sound Effects: Music

Sound Effects: Music

Sound Effects: Music

Sound Effects: Music

Cut to shot of LML staring and moving on its own.
Sound Effects: Music

Sound Effects: Music

The film ends with the man appreciating the scooter.
VO: Style. Power. Performance
LML VESPA

it was launched, LML Vespa had garnered a 23 per cent market share, up from 5 per cent in 1988, while Bajaj and Kinetic Honda had both dropped shares in a market growing at 8 per cent, from 79 per cent and 10 per cent to 68 per cent and 9 per cent respectively.

The success of LML Vespa is a classic example of how a late entrant in a market dominated by a giant, was able to carve a significant share for itself by following a few basic rules:

- Don't attack the market leader head-on, especially when it enjoys a near monopoly status in the market.
- Ensure that your brand has a distinct identity and position of its own that can't be appropriated by anybody else, especially by the market leader.
- Write your own rules, don't let others define the rules of the game.

LML Vespa: Brand Building Tips

When taking on the market leader, build a positioning for your brand that cannot be appropriated by the leader. LML Vespa could look at Bajaj and discover a weakness that was waiting to be exploited. The 'style-power-performance' platform helped LML Vespa establish a strong position against the 'trust' position of Bajaj.

(Case based on the presentation made at Bombay Advertising Club's Ad-Works Seminar, 1997.)

VOLTAS MEGA LAUNDRETTE—Only Size Matters

The boom in the white goods (comprising refrigeration and washing machines) industry started in the late 1980s. Ever since then the industry has not looked back. Today, the industry accounts for more than Rs 48 billion and is growing at the rate of 15–20 per cent per annum (p.a.). Various factors ranging from higher aspirational levels, changing lifestyles, rapid urbanisation, the increasing pace of life, growth of the middle class and liberalisation of the economy fuelled the revolution in the industry.

THE WASHING MACHINE MARKET

Of all the segments in the white goods category, the washing machine market has perhaps been the slowest to take off. When the first washing machine was launched in the mid 1980s, it found few takers. But in the mid 1990s, the washing machine market had become as competitive as the refrigerator and the television markets.

The washing machine market in India is split into three segments operating in three distinct price bands: washers/manual washing machines in the Rs 3,000–5000 range, semi-automatic (SA) washing machines ranging from Rs 6,000–9,500 and fully automatic (FA) washing machines available for anything between Rs 15,000–Rs 30,000 depending upon their features.

Washing Machine Market

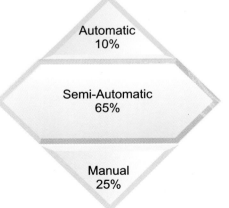

Automatic 10%

Semi-Automatic 65%

Manual 25%

The size of the washing machine market in 1995 was estimated at almost 6,00,000 units, valued at Rs 5,750 mm with a growth rate of 25 per cent per annum. Of the three segments, semi-automatic machines accounted for 65 per cent; washers/manual machines for 25 per cent and fully-automatic machines for 10 per cent. Market trends indicated that while the washers/manual machine segment was declining, the semi-automatic and fully automatic machine segments were growing at 30 per cent and 50 per cent respectively.

This was attributed to an upward shift from washers to semi-automatics and semi-automatics to fully automatic washing machines, and an increase in purchasing power and affluence levels. Clearly, the washing machine market was poised for growth and was going to be akin to what the TV/refrigerator markets had been in the late 1980s and early 1990s.

Home Durables Hierarchy

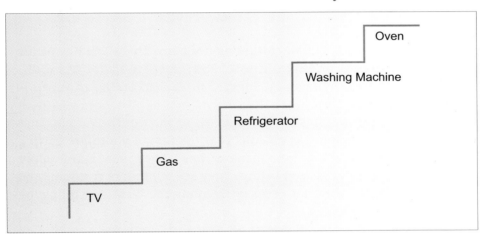

One of the key reasons for the low all-India penetration of washing machines (1.8 per cent) as compared to television sets (22 per cent) and refrigerators (9.1 per cent) was that the washing machine was seen as more of a luxury, and thus featured way behind a television set or a refrigerator in the consumer's consideration list. Furthermore, its usage was confined to metros and large towns due to non-availability of running water and electricity in other areas.

Competitive Scenario

The washing machine market began to grow in the mid 1990s with a vengeance. Although the market was not expected to be as large as the television or the refrigerator market, it offered marketeers both volume and value. Videocon was the first to enter the market with other white

THE NEXT GENERATION

India celebrated 50 years of its freedom in 1997. The entire generation that is emerging now has no memories of the freedom struggle–in some cases it is twice removed from the freedom movement.

A study done across 10 cities amongst today's youngsters (18-22 years) presents an interesting picture.

In spite of the TV invasion, the Indian youth present an interesting picture of contradictions. In fact 81.8% of the youth felt that they would not hurt their parents by marrying against their wishes; while 49.9% maintain that they are free to marry outside their community. While 41% disapprove of government censorship of movies, 65% disapprove of public display of affection.

Indian youth today see Indian culture as not being threatened by MNCs (20%), satellite TV (22%), beauty contests (25%), foreign magazines (30%) or MTV/Channel V (38%). The single biggest threat, according to them, is explicit sex in movies (79%).

If we layer this on the present day worries of the youth like entrance exams, future—job—career, it is obvious that the Indian youth are getting more focused than the previous generations. They see many more opportunities where none existed before. They see a lot more freedom. And they want to do it their way, not necessarily aping the West, nor following the footsteps of their fathers.

How will this change over the next 50 years? As India gets integrated more and more into the global economic mainstream, will Indian youth also change? Only time will tell.

Source: Times of India, Bombay, September 6, 1998
Times of India, Bombay, August 8, 1997

good consumer durables, with many major companies following suit–IFB Bosch, BPL, TVS, Onida, Godrej, Sumeet and a host of others.

Since the top-end offered the highest growth, every marketeer focused his marketing efforts on the fully automatic and the semi-automatic segments. On offer was almost every product type, offering features ranging from front and top loading, cold and hot wash, fuzzy logic machines that thought for themselves, with innumerable wash programmes that allowed the consumer to decide upon the kind of wash, the time when she wanted to do her washing etc.

BRAND BUILDING ADVERTISING ■

Poster
Voltas Mega Laundrette
"Men take performance..."

This resulted in a very high degree of similarity of product looks and features, with little or no differentiation among them, leaving the consumer hard-pressed for a reason to buy a particular brand. In the end, it came down to how much of noise each brand created in the market-place and the overall image of the brand and the company.

Videocon dominated the market with a market share of 46 per cent with a significant presence in all the three segments, followed by BPL and TVS Whirlpool with 19 per cent and 12 per cent respectively. Other players were IFB (8 per cent), Onida (5 per cent), Godrej (4 per cent), Sumeet and Maharaja. Unlike Videocon which was present in all the segments, most brands were present in the automatic and semi-automatic segments.

The Entry of Voltas

It was against such a background that Voltas decided to enter the washing machine market. Voltas was no stranger to the white goods market. It had a formidable presence in the air-conditioning and refrigeration segments where it enjoyed the number one and number three positions respectively. Voltas had entered into a tie-up with the Korean giant, Samsung, for manufacturing and marketing washing machines in the domestic market. Voltas had targeted the semi- and fully automatic machine segments with three models with wash capacities ranging between 5 kg and 5.5 kg, the largest in their category at that time.

Voltas already had its distribution network in place due to its presence in the refrigerator and air-conditioning segments, and had a strong equity among the trade and consumers.

Despite this, Voltas suffered from a disadvantage. It was the tenth national brand to enter the washing machine market with a product similar to other brands and ran the risk of being perceived as a "me-too" brand.

Query Line

Q. In advertising agencies creative, and at times servicing and planning teams, spend time watching movies because:

- It is a good 'timepass' activity
- It helps 'bonding' among teams
- It stimulates thinking.

Ans. Advertising derives its ideas from life and all that life throws up, especially the creative arts. So advertising professionals spend time, even 'office' time watching movies, paintings, photography and fiction books, because these activities stimulate creative thinking.

The Objective and Strategy

Given this scenario, Voltas defined its objective as being seen as a brand with the latest, premium products on par with international technology and offering the widest possible range. To achieve its objective, Voltas realised that it had to synergize every element of its marketing effort and leverage its leadership image in refrigeration and air-conditioning to gain an entry into the washing machine market.

Competitive Scenario

- Product

An evaluation of the different products revealed that except for the front loading machines (IFB Bosch and Sumeet were the only players with this mode), all machines looked alike, had similar wash capacities and had more or less the same features, resulting in low product differentiation and making the marketing task more difficult.

Competitive Scenario

- Price

It was observed that while washers and semi-automatic washing machines operated in tight price bands, the fully automatic machine was available in a wide band which would enable the product to command a premium.

Competitive Scenario

• Advertising

A scan of competitive advertising revealed that all brands emphasised the features. It was very likely that ad spends would increase by as much as 40–50 per cent making it virtually impossible for Voltas to consider a dominating share of voice. An evaluation of the competitive advertising revealed that all of them tried to appropriate the 'wash/clean' property such as 'pressure cleaning'=BPL; 'technoclean'=Videocon; 'agitator wash'=TVS; 'power wash'=Godrej and others.

All the brands promised superior cleaning and assured the customer that they offered a gentle wash.

Consumer Tracking

The agency felt that the solution to the problem lay with the consumer, and that it was not just a matter of saying what the competition was saying in a better manner.

In-depth interviews and focus group discussions were conducted among users of both semi-automatic and fully automatic machines. The findings indicated a re-definition in the role of the housewife. From a self-

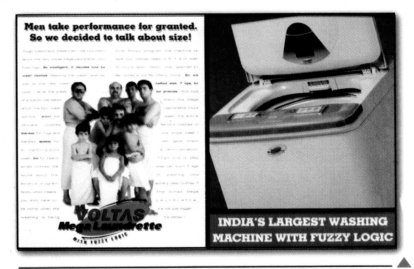

Poster Ad
Voltas Mega Laundrette
"Men take performance for granted..."

sacrificing martyr, she had evolved into an individual with a unique identity of her own. A washing machine gave her the freedom and flexibility from the daily drudgery and allowed her to spend time with her family. Since she sought objects offering utility and convenience a washing machine for her was a necessity and not a luxury.

Housewise Typologies

Old	Emerging
'Sacrifice for the family'	'I want my family to be happy'
'Living for the family'	'I want the best possible for my family'
'My time is family time'	'My time is valuable'
'I need to do it myself'	'I need to do only the important things myself'
'I should save as much as possible'	

The washing habits and patterns indicated that the frequency of machine wash depended upon the size of the household, type of clothes washed in the machine—daily use clothes, linens, towels, etc. were washed in the machine, while delicate clothes like silks, blends etc. were invariably hand-washed or dry-cleaned. The machine was used when the load of clothes piled up; interestingly the load size was measured by the number of clothes, estimated through experience and was not a translation of the washing capacity of the machine.

Certain negatives, however, still existed. It was felt that by using washing machines, clothes wore out faster, cuffs and collars did not come out clean and that a hot wash/laundry wash was necessary for clothes at regular intervals. The consumer, however, was willing to compromise on these because of the convenience, the washing machine offered.

Another interesting set of findings that emerged was that clothes needed to be pre-soaked even for a machine wash to ensure a clean wash and that a laundry wash was the best, as it offered the cleanest wash. An analysis of the buying process indicated that while the housewife initiated the process and acted as an influencer, the final decision was made by the male on technical parameters. Unlike the male, the woman sought a machine that was user-friendly and gave a quality wash.

Heard-in-the-Agency

(Amusing exchanges between 'anxious' servicing and even more 'anxious' creative folks.)

"All right, it's not the full page we promised you.

So you've got to cut copy by no more than 95%.

I don't see the problem.

How much space did it take Shakespeare to say:

" To be or not to be!"

Heh, heh, just a little humour."

The Strategy

● Umbrella

In a market over-crowded with brands, models and multiple options, how could one create a difference—this was the challenge-facing Voltas.

It was obvious that Voltas would have to introduce a range of models to take care of the specific need gaps/segments in the market. But the first issue was to identify the one brand promise that would cut across the model options.

Consumer research had thrown up several interesting nuggets, such as, "Nothing is better than laundry wash," "I still remember the spotless cleaning of laundry."

Was there something that Voltas could appropriate, and use across modes? If so, how could it make it a Voltas property?

Thus was born the 'Laundrette' brand name that was given to all the Voltas washing machines. The range was now distinguishable with a relevant brand name: Voltas Laundrette.

The brand name tested very well, with consumers saying that it meant clothes will come out 'clean', 'laundry clean' from a Voltas washing machine.

Voltas had a whole range of models to offer. The next question was: which model should it push?

● Model

A number of options emerged. The first was to promote the whole range as 'the Laundrette series/range'. This would not have cut through the clutter and was quickly abandoned. The next option was to identify two or three key models and promote all of them aggressively. This meant that a large budget outlay was needed so that each model got sufficient inputs to break through the clutter.

Finally, it was decided that Voltas had to gain image leadership over the large brands. This could be achieved if Voltas took its top-of-the-line model and made it the image leader for the entire range.

The choice fed upon the premium model, which was fuzzy-logic with numerous wash options and with the largest wash capacity, 7 kg, in its class. This model was named Voltas Mega Laundrette and advertising was to be developed to promote this model.

Voltas Mega Laundrette: Positioning

The Voltas Mega Laundrette offered all the benefits and features offered by the leading brands. In short, it was a top-of-the-line product. Now which feature should be played up? Competitors were harping on numerous high-tech benefits. Could Voltas cut a different path?

Market analysis revealed that Voltas Mega Laundrette offered a 7 kg wash capacity— not matched by most other models. Could 'capacity' be the difference?

In a market overcrowded with electronic wizardry, 'capacity' became temptingly simple. It was a relevant benefit and if handled rightly, could help Voltas offer everything that all other top-line models offered plus capacity.

The Voltas Mega Laundrette was positioned as "the Largest Washing Machine in its class".

Creative Execution

The creative challenge was to promote capacity without making it sound trivial or low-tech. The creative brief got the team sparkling with ideas.

The Creative Brief

Single-Minded Proposition	: Voltas Mega Laundrette is the largest capacity state-of-the-art washing machine in India.
Support for the Proposition	: 7 kg wash capacity : can wash up to 7 trousers, 4 sarees, 7 shirts, 3 T. Shirts, 5 shorts, 15 undergarments.
	: All the top-end state-of-the-art features like wash options etc. are there in Voltas Mega Laundrette.

The creative breakthrough came with the idea of eight men in towels waiting for their clothes to get washed!

How could this be made different and still enjoyable as a television script?

This led to the white-on-white treatment, a jingle without any musical instruments and a challenge feed by the lady of the house vis-a-vis her extended joint family consisting of old men, young men and children!

Voltas Mega Laundrette

Film opens on men of a family standing wearing bath towels.
One man sings: 'This is not possible'.

Voltas Mega Laundrette appears.
Lady of the house: 'My new Voltas Mega Laundrette...'

The little girl now appears on the screen.
Girl: 'We're done with the clothes. Now towels, please.'

Cut to one man from the group singing loudly.
Another joins in: 'Just not possible'.

WVO: '....Can wash clothes for the entire family.'

Visibly shocked men, now hold on to their towels.

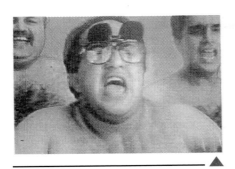

Cut to another man still singing loudly.
Together: 'No single washing machine can wash so many clothes.'

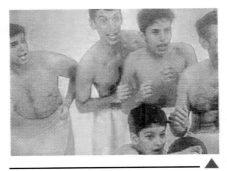

Sound Effects: Music

The execution stayed away from all claims made by other brands and went about its task singlemindedly. It featured eight men and two children clad in white towels to suggest that their clothes had gone for a wash. To throw up the challenge that the machine could possibly not wash all their clothes at one go, they break out into a song, with each member voicing his opinion about the impossibility of the task.

At the start of the song the little girl, a member of the troupe, slips away, only to return later to tell the men, "The clothes have been washed, now the towels go in", leaving the men flabbergasted and frantically clutching their towels!

The television commercial was followed through with press advertising and merchandising support. Interesting, large cut-out merchandising material literally brought the commercial into every showroom.

RESULTS

The television commercial was an instant hit. It got customers visiting showrooms asking for the Voltas Mega Laundrette. Voltas suddenly became a salient brand, in spite of being the tenth entrant into the washing machine market.

The increased brand salience led to the entire range benefiting, as was expected, making Voltas one of the top brands within a year of its launch.

The advertising of Voltas Mega Laundrette is a true example of focused strategy and creative breakthrough going on to build brand sales in a record short period!

Voltas Mega Laundrette: Brand Building Tips

In a crowded category, it is useful to identify a benefit hitherto unexploited by the competition. The advertising should then focus on that benefit–promise and blow it up to giant proportions. Voltas Mega Laundrette focused its energies on 'large capacity' and broke through the clutter of washing machine advertising.

CASE STUDY

USHA SEWING MACHINES: Building a Gem Collection

Staging a comeback in a competitive market when the competition is one up on you is difficult, especially so when the market leader, by virtue of being the pioneer, is involved in the same activity that you are in. The task becomes even more difficult when there is stiff competition from a large unorganised sector, offering a similar product, constantly sniffing at your heels as well.

But there are companies which have utilised their expertise and strengths to make a comeback. Usha is one such company which has managed to create a competitive edge for itself to stage a remarkable recovery in the marketplace.

THE MARKET

The Indian sewing machine market traces its roots to 1871, when Singer came to India, 20 years after Isaac Merritt Singer invented the first practical sewing machine. The indigenous manufacture of sewing machines would however, commence only in the early 1940s. By then, Singer which was the pioneer, had found its way into numerous homes and its name had become synonymous with sewing.

Until the early 1980s, most of the machines that were manufactured were of the traditional black-round-arm variety which can do simple, straight stitching. The industry growth had been sluggish, ranging between 3 per cent and 4 per cent.

Although precise figures are unavailable, it is estimated that the current size of the market is around Rs 15 billion, made up of 1.4 million units—including sales of the organised and unorganised sectors. Since the manufacture of sewing machines is reserved for the small scale sector, the industry has hardly witnessed any modernisation.

The Competition

There are two national players—Usha and Singer, eight regional players, over 300 local brands and a very large unorganised sector that make up the bulk of the sewing machine market. The two national players account forasmuch as 80 per cent of the organised market; but only 45 per cent of the total market, with the unorganised sector and regional players accounting for 45 per cent and 10 per cent respectively.

Sewing Machine Market

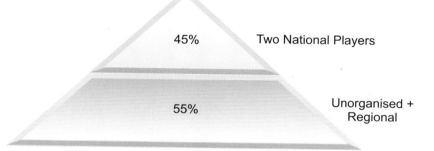

45%   Two National Players

55%   Unorganised + Regional

The retail price of a hand machine of a national brand ranges between Rs 800 – Rs 1400 depending upon the model. The regional brands are between 10–18 per cent lower, while local brands are 25–35 per cent less expensive than the national brands.

Stagnation

Usha, which is also actively present in other home appliances segmants like fans, geysers etc. faced stagnation in the sales of sewing machines towards the 1980s. Apart from the fact that there was virtually no replacement market, there were other larger problems. Not so long ago, the sewing machine was high in the consumers, consideration list of household purchases. But with the arrival of a host of new consumer electronic and convenience goods, it had slipped down the priority list.

At another level, with ready-made garments gaining increasing acceptance, dependence on sewing machines had reduced. Also, there was a growing perception among the higher income groups that sewing was a drudgery. This was a problem that affected both Usha and Singer the most.

Until the mid 1980s, Usha was clearly the market leader, ahead of Singer with a 23 per cent market share. In 1985, Singer introduced a top-

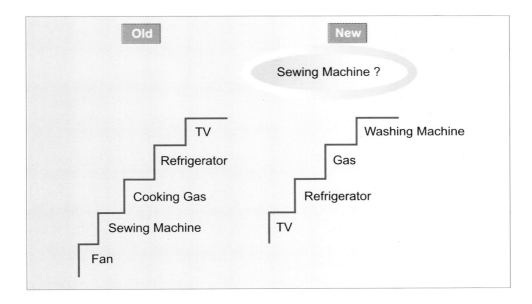

of-the-line automatic zigzag sewing machine under the 'Singer Fashion Maker' brand name. In the meantime, it had also evolved a three brand strategy catering to the price-conscious consumer, the brand-conscious consumer and the fashion-conscious consumer. These were marketed in rural and urban markets under the Regnis, Merritt and Singer brand names. This enabled Singer to consolidate its position in the three different segments. The introduction of the automatic zigzag machine, 'Singer Fashion Maker', saw the top-end witnessing impressive growth, with Singer's sales overtaking that of Usha.

Although Usha had been in the market with a zigzag model, it was unrepresented in the automatic segment and had been unable to make much headway with it in the decorative stitching segment. Furthermore, there was no product differentiation in its medium and lower level machines. As a result, Usha found itself under pressure from Singer at the top-end and from the regional brands and the unorganised sector at the bottom end.

Under increasing pressure in the marketplace, Usha called in its agency, FCB-Ulka to design a communication strategy for its brand of sewing machines to arrest the decline in its sales.

The Consumer

Research showed that as many as 84 per cent of sewing machines purchasers were between 22 and 45 years old. Almost 70 per cent used the sewing machine as a pastime to stitch clothes for themselves and their

INDIAS' PERCEPTION OF MONEY

Indians are among the world's biggest savers' of money. Our saving rate has always been very high. We also worship money, in the form of Goddess Lakshmi.

A survey conducted by Sofres-MODE across seven cities, reveals some interesting highlights, that further confirm this hypothesis.

Indians consider money to be the most important thing in life (38%), followed by job security (31%), fame (16%), power (11%) and other factors (4%). Among the younger lot, job security scores higher and among the 60+ age group, it's money above all.

So what would they do with the surplus money? Well the overwhelming response is: save it (73%). It is amazing that this opinion is almost unchanged across various age groups.

More than half, (55%), claim to have a long term investment plan, but only 57% prepare a monthly budget.

Saving habits get dictated by the investment climate, and quite predictably in 1998, saving options were skewed towards the 'perceived' low risk options: Savings bank (35%), Fixed Deposits (27%), Property (21%), Gold (11%), Chit fund (4%), Stock/Shares (2%).

The attitude towards credit is changing but we are still a far cry from becoming a credit driven economy. Almost half the people consider credit to be an option only for the purchase of a house! (The pioneering work done by the Housing Development Finance Corporation (HDFC) is reflected in consumer attitudes). Again almost half the people believe that buying household items on credit is not a sensible thing.

Obviously Indians are very value-driven and careful about their money. The youth may be more amenable to attractive 'credit' options rather than the 40+ age group. However, even they will need some pushing!

Source: Intelligent Investor
August 26, 1998

family. Only 30 per cent, used it to bolster household income by stitching clothes for others.

The buying process is normally initiated by the wife but the brand selection and final purchase are jointly done by the husband and wife. A sewing machine is a once-in-a-life-time purchase and the buying process takes between two and three months—involving information gathering, com-parison of features and prices, brand image, mode of purchase and the like.

Research

To gain a clear understanding of Usha's status in the marketplace, FCB-Ulka undertook a research study on the image of Usha vis-à-vis Singer.

Research showed that Singer was increasingly being seen as providing greater value in terms of (a) changing with the times, (b) having a contemporary image and (c) having the latest technology, courtesy, the Singer Fashion Maker.

Usha, on the other hand, was seen as old-fashioned and re-presenting old values, while providing no value addition whatsoever.

An analysis of the study indicated that the brand needed a more contemporary image and had to provide value-addition to the existing product range. This was easier said than done since product upgradation by way of addition of new product features was not possible in the short term. It was clear that Usha could not wait for the upgradation of its product range to counter Singer's offensive, and that communications and advertising would have to start delivering immediately to prevent Singer and other players from eating into Usha's share of the market.

The Solution

After a lot of brainstorming sessions, both internally and with the marketing team at Usha, the team arrived at the brand strategy to be followed for Usha sewing machines.

The agency-client team believed that until Usha could get its manufacturing infrastructure in place, its advertising would have to start delivering immediately to prevent Singer and other players from eating

Query Line

Q. While creating advertising for a premium durable brand it is necessary to ensure that:
- It is very rational
- It is very emotional
- It is a blend of both

Ans. Premium durables could be in the form of a washing machine, a car or a watch. While they are all high involvement products and will call for a fair amount of 'rational' thinking, they cannot be bereft of any 'emotional' hooks. Hence best premium durable advertising has a blend of both, a bit more of rational sometimes and a bit more of emotional at times!

into Usha's share of the market. The team believed that the first step was in refurbishing the existing product range so as to give it a more contemporary look and image.

Accordingly, all the models were revamped in terms of styling and colours. From being a dull, purely functional product, Usha's range of sewing machines underwent a metamorphosis, becoming gleaming, sleek and colourful machines that took one's breath away.

Not to be left behind was the branding of the new range of Usha sewing machines. In keeping with its contemporary looks and image and the brand values that Usha represented, the range was branded as '*The Gem Collection*'. The creative concept was developed keeping in mind the brand name and the values that Usha had over the years come to stand for: 'A contemporary fashion statement rooted in premium quality and good value'.

The Advertising

The advertising campaign comprised press advertisements for release in dailies and women's magazines, in addition to a few general interest magazines to target the husband as well. The press campaign featured product shots and displayed the entire range of sewing machines. In addition, point of sale material was developed—comprising posters and attractive danglers—as an extension of the press campaign.

The Launch and the Response

The new range of Usha sewing machines under the brand name "The Gem Collection" was initially test marketed in Kanpur and Bangalore. Two-and-a-half months after the formal launch, the agency undertook an image study to evaluate the effectiveness of the communication and the brand's status in the marketplace. The findings indicated that Usha's standing vis-à-vis Singer improved dramatically across all parameters.

Usha Sewing Machine—Golden Pearl

VO: For today's woman.

VO: A modern sewing machine.

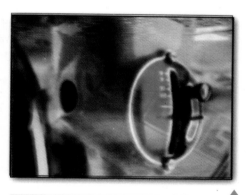

The film is a series of shots of a well dressed lady interspersed with product shots.

VO: New Golden Pearl.

VO: From Usha's Gem Collection.

Sound Effects: Music

Usha Sewing Machine—Star Sapphire

VO: *For today's woman.*

VO: *A modern sewing machine.*

The film is a series of shots of a well dressed lady interspersed with product shots.

VO: *From Usha's Gem Collection.*

VO: *New Star Sapphire.*

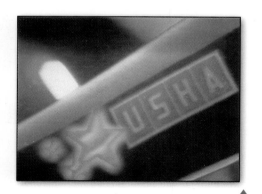

Sound Effects: Music

Press Ad
Usha Sewing Machine
"Presenting a flawless performer..."

Press Ad
Usha Sewing Machine
"Years later you'll still..."

Press Ad
Usha Sewing Machine
"You'll treasure its beauty..."

Image Score Track

Centre: Kanpur	1991			1992		
	Usha	Singer	Usha Singer	Usha	Singer	Usha Singer
1. Modernity	5.6	5.8	-0.2	5.9	4.4	1.5
2. Attractive	8.6	8.4	0.2	8.8	6.9	1.9
3. Technology	6.6	6.2	0.4	7.3	5.6	1.7
4. Keeps pace with the times	8.8	8.6	0.2	8.6	6.9	1.7
5. Brings out new models	9.0	9.0	—	7.4	5.4	2.0
Centre : Bangalore						
1. Modernity	4.8	7.0	-2.2	5.8	6.4	-0.6
2. Attractive	8.8	8.4	0.4	8.9	7.7	1.2
3. Technology	7.0	7.4	-0.4	6.3	6.9	-0.6
4. Keeps pace with the times	7.6	7.8	-0.2	7.3	6.7	0.6
5. Brings out new models	7.0	7.4	-0.4	7.3	6.7	0.4

Following the positive consumer acceptance, Usha's Gem Collection was rolled out nationally. Overall brand sales, which were stagnating earlier, began to show an upward trend. More encouraging, from the company's point of view, was the increase in the proportion of sales among its various models. The sales, especially of its premium priced models grew by 254 per cent, indicating the entry of new users and upgradation from its standard and economy models.

In the meantime, Usha has been busy on other fronts as well. Its distribution network has been expanded dramatically—the company had always relied on a mix of exclusive showrooms and multi-brand outlets, as a result of which its reach has improved considerably. Determined efforts have been made to sustain public interest in sewing, especially in the small towns and semi-urban areas. This has been done in the form of sewing schools where women are taught sewing skills. The next part of the programme is to increase the number of such schools across the country and to introduce higher-end models to counter Singer's Fashion Maker and increase its franchise in the market-place.

This case study of Usha sewing machines goes to show how a company can re-energize a brand in a sluggish market through focused brand building efforts. The approach of creating a sub-brand and using it to add lustre to the parent brand has now been adopted by many durable marketeers.

> ## Usha Gem Collection: Brand Building Tips
>
> It is often possible to energize even a declining product category by changing the orientation of the category. Usha could achieve this through the use of an interesting sub-brand that looked different and spelled 'style' 'new' to a tired consumer, achieving breakthrough success.

GODREJ STORWEL—Selling an Emotion

There are brands and then there are brands. The former are those that follow the traditional product lifecycle. From the launch stage, they go through the consecutive stages of growth, maturity and decline, dying a natural death. Then again, there are those that endure the test of time. These are brands that become generic to the category, like Nylon, Cellophane, Scotch tape, Xerox etc. Closer home, the Godrej Storwel steel cupboard is a classic example of this phenomenon.

The success of Godrej Storwel is all the more remarkable considering that in a market where competitive brands are available at almost half its price, it is the largest selling brand. A measure of the brand's strength is that in today's world of instant gratification, where everything is wanted immediately, consumers are willingly to pay anything between Rs 8,000 and Rs 14,000 upfront and wait for a minimum of 4-6 weeks for delivery.

THE BEGINNING

In 1897, a young lawyer gave up his profession and took up lock-making. His name was Ardeshir Burjorjee Godrej. A staunch nationalist, he realised that for India to become self-sufficient and self-reliant, it would have to manufacture its own goods to compete with and displace the foreign brands that dominated the market. This, he believed, would be achieved only by offering the consumer reliable, quality products at reasonable rates.

The first batch of Godrej locks were made in 1897. The success of the product confirmed Ardeshir Godrej's belief that an Indian product could successfully compete with foreign brands, if it offered the consumer quality and reliability. From locks, Ardeshir moved on to the manufacture of safes, many of which are still in use today, a natural and logical extension from lock-making.

The Godrej vision was a fundamental one—a commitment to basic human values and to the highest standards of reliability and quality. This was the basis and the starting point; diversification into other businesses was the necessary expression of a broader perspective.

Pirojsha B. Godrej, was a worthy successor to his brother, Ardeshir B. Godrej. If the latter laid the foundations, Pirojsha B. Godrej was responsible for building and expanding the vast industrial empire that Godrej is today. Taking cues from the changing times and adapting to changes in the environment, Godrej diversified into other lines such as the manufacture of office equipment and steel furniture, which it pioneered, among others.

In the late 1930s and early 1940s, the steel cupboard came into its own as a product category in India. Until then, valuables were invariably stored in steel safes and other items in wooden cupboards. The steel cupboard changed all that, offering the consumer a better alternative for his storage requirements. The ease of manufacture and low production costs led to the mushrooming of scores of small time entrepreneurs setting up production units in the backyards of their homes. All that one needed was a skilled ironmonger/smith, a welding machine and some steel. However, most of these cupboards were of poor quality and left a lot to be desired.

Sensing the potential that the market offered, Godrej, which had already established a strong reputation for its range of locks and safes diversified into the manufacture of steel cupboards. A large plant was set up in the industrial township of Vikhroli in Bombay for the production of steel cupboards.

THE MARKET

Come 1980. The market for steel cupboards is highly fragmented, with the manufacture of steel cupboards dotted across the length and breadth of the country. The mushrooming and dominance of the unorganized sector is primarily due to lower material manufacturing costs and evasion of duties and taxes. Of the 2.8 million odd pieces sold annually, the organized sector accounts for a mere 10 per cent of the market, which is growing at 6 to 8 per cent annually. The organized sector largely comprises regional brands and there are only two national brands, viz. Godrej and Allwyn (the latter was re-launched in November 1996).

Priced at 25-40 per cent below regional brands and as much as 80–100 per cent below Godrej, with matching features to boot, the unorganised sector enjoys a strong competitive edge in terms of pricing.

The market for steel cupboards is primarily divided into the home and office segments. Of the two, the home segment accounts for as much as 60–70 per cent of total sales and exhibits a high degree of seasonality with sales peaking during the festival and marriage seasons (August to

November and February to May respectively). The sale of cupboards in the office/institutional segment, that accounts for the balance, is more or less constant throughout the year. Although the office/institutional segment has been gradually declining due to the increasing use of modular office furniture, the overall market is growing at 8–10 per cent per annum primarily due to the growth in the home segment.

GODREJ STORWEL

Ever since the first batch rolled out of the plant in 1943, the Godrej cupboards found ready acceptance in the marketplace. Made from superior steel which was specially treated for corrosion, the cupboards were of flawless construction with a locker for valuables and a provision of adjustable shelves, and were undoubtedly the best cupboards in the market. Furthermore, the equity enjoyed by Godrej locks and safes helped. The Godrej name was synonymous with quality and reliability; the now famous Godrej signature that appeared on every product was a visible assurance of these values to the consumer.

Pirojsha B. Godrej believed that a quality product alone did not make for success. He held that product availability, branding, a strong and effective distribution system and advertising were key elements in the success of a product.

The first step was the setting up of branch offices in all major cities from where order bookings were taken from customers. The distribution network was further strengthened by the addition of authorised dealers, exclusive company showrooms as well as multi-brand retail outlets.

The steel cupboards did not need much advertising initially. The product's quality spoke for itself and with the market growing at a rapid pace, sales of the Godrej cupboard grew as time went by. With a fairly large distribution network in place, product availability was not a problem and the company sold whatever quantity it produced, largely on the equity of the Godrej name.

The visionary that he was, Pirojsha Godrej was only too aware of the difference that advertising would make between a has-been and a market leader. Unlike others, he viewed advertising as an investment and not as expenditure. In 1963, the newly formed agency, FCB-Ulka Advertising, was signed on to handle the advertising for Godrej's range of office equipment, furniture and cupboards.

Brand Strategy

Among the measures recommended was branding the product as Godrej Storwel. 'Storwel' was chosen, for it strongly cued the product as a superior storage system in comparison to other steel cupboards. The Godrej name was retained for the values of 'quality, durability, reliability and value for money' that it stood for. The positioning or rather its USP was rooted in the product's attribute of superior quality and offered the consumer durability and value for money. The initial advertising spoke of the superiority of the Godrej cupboard vis-à-vis other cupboards and highlighted the various product features, many of which were firsts in the category. With the growth in the economy, the office/institutional segment was targeted through advertising and institutional selling, a move that paid rich dividends.

The strategy paid off and sales of Godrej Storwel grew. Over time, its distribution network was further strengthened to increase reach with the addition of exclusive and multi-brand outlets spanning the length and breadth of the country. By the end of the 1970s, it had become the largest selling brand of steel cupboards in the country.

The 1980s

As consumer acceptance grew, so did the competition in the form of the unorganised sector and regional players. With easy availability of technology, the competition had spruced up its act. They also enjoyed a strong price advantage due to low manufacturing overheads as a result of zero duties and taxes and by outsourcing components and/or the whole product. Unlike them, Godrej's production was completely in-house to ensure quality standards. Furthermore, the duties and taxes formed a large component of the production costs. As a result of this, Godrej was not able to lower its prices to match those of the competition.

Although Godrej's sales were not affected due to its strong equity among consumers and the market's high growth rate, it was a cause for concern.

In the early 1980s, faced with competition from small players, the agency undertook a study among consumers to identify attitudes and beliefs about Godrej Storwel. The findings revealed that the Godrej Storwel enjoyed a strong equity among consumers. The existing users of Godrej Storwel swore by it; the second cupboard purchased was always a Storwel. It was found that a cupboard featured actively in the consumers' consideration list and that Godrej Storwel was the reference brand. The purchase of a cupboard was need-based. Being a high value, high involvement product, the decision was taken jointly between the husband and wife with friends, relatives and dealers acting as influencers.

It was found that the most common occasions for purchase were marriage, birth of a child and when setting up a home.

In the office segment as well, Godrej Storwel enjoyed a high degree of equity and was seen as the best steel cupboard available because of its superior quality and product features. Furthermore, while the purchase of an ordinary cupboard was usually met with raised eyebrows that hinted of underhand dealings, a Storwel was above suspicion.

The 1990s

By the early 1990s, Godrej was selling all of the 1,20,000 units it was producing annually, making it the largest selling brand of steel cupboards in the country. Despite this, Godrej found itself losing market share in a growing market. The main causes for this were Godrej's limited production capacity, growing competition, changes in the consumers' lifestyle, consumer perception related problems and a delivery period of a minimum of 4–6 weeks.

The 1990s witnessed a sea change in the consumer's habits and lifestyles. With the communications explosion and increasing consumer affluence levels, cupboards no longer featured actively on the consumers' hierarchy of needs, coming way below other items like refrigerators, TVs, audio systems etc. Furthermore, with competition offering similar cupboards with identical features to boot, priced 25–80 per cent below that of a Godrej Storwel, promising immediate delivery as well, the consumer was able to spread his capital over two durables. This gave the first time user a reason to buy a cheaper alternative to a Godrej Storwel.

Despite its limited production capacity, Godrej was unwilling to farm out production of its cupboards to outside suppliers. This was primarily due to its fear of losing control over the quality of the end product. Further, the aesthetics of the Godrej Storwel remained unchanged over the years which did not help either. Despite manufacturing upgradations, changes in the manufacturing process and raw materials were seen in a negative light by consumers who thought that Godrej was cutting corners and compromising on the quality of the product.

The situation was compounded further by the time taken to deliver. In a market scenario where the consumer could take home a durable like a TV or a refrigerator immediately, the Godrej customer had to wait a minimum of 4–6 weeks for delivery, after having paid for the Storwel upfront. This delay in delivery put off many potential users who would invariably purchase a competitive brand.

The only heartening factor was that despite these adverse conditions, Godrej was continuing to sell all the 1,20,000 units it manufactured with a minimum of another 20,000 orders pending at the end of the year. Clearly the brand had a lot of potential in it.

The 1995 Study

The agency undertook a study in 1995 to identify consumer attitudes and the motivating factors that made consumers purchase more than 1,20,000 Storwels despite all the difficulties that they had to go through.

In-depth interviews were conducted among 250 respondents in 7 centres, all of whom were recent buyers of Godrej Storwel. The findings indicated that Godrej Storwel meant more than just storage space to the consumer. For him, Godrej Storwel meant safety, security, trust and reliability–values which stemmed from its image leadership, product quality and its strong equity. The key motivating factor was a sense of security associated with the brand. "I can't trust my valuables to any ordinary steel cupboard. Nothing but a Godrej Storwel will do", was the near universal response received in the study.

Advertising History

Godrej Storwel was the generic steel cupboard. The brand advertising for several decades was focused on better quality and better reliability.

When the brand came under serious attack in the 1980s, there was a need for a paradigm shift.

The lower priced competitors offered a very similar looking product. Given the fact that there were no moving parts, wear and tear was very minimum. Hence a local brand lasted a long time, unlike most other product categories.

The consumer understood that Godrej was using better steel, better locks, better hinges etc. But he was not sure that all that merited a large extra payment.

Advertising had to do more than just sell rational reasons, because just the brand name Godrej Storwel said it all.

Consumer interviews gave interesting clues:

- "Godrej Storwel came when I got married."
- "It is almost like a family member."
- "I bought another one for baby's clothes."
- "In our family it has come down two generations."

Godrej Storwel was more than a mere cupboard. It was a part of Indian families. This led to a series of very successful television commercials in the 1980s:

'Marriage': This jingle-based commercial shows a new *bahu* entering her house (husband's) for the first time in her life and being given the keys to her own Godrej Storwel. The brand implicitly promises a 'happier future'.

'Baby': This film shows mother coming home with her new born to be greeted by her elder one who has labelled the Godrej Storwel as "Baby" "Me". Again ending with the tag line of 'happier homes'.

'Brothers': This has two brothers fighting over shelf space in a Godrej Storwel, till the fight is broken by the smaller chap getting his own storwel for his birthday!

The three commercials ran for a long period and helped Godrej Storwel build a strong emotional bond with its consumers.

In 1995 research once again got consumers talking about these commercials, even though they had been off the air for three years!

Was there something in those commercials that Godrej could capitalise on?

Creative Execution: 1995

The 'Marriage' commercial of Storwel was etched in the collective psyche of the country. It was time that Storwel went back to dig up those memories.

From here was born the idea for a commercial based on another Indian custom—celebration of a 'would be mother'. Motherhood is seen as the ultimate test of womanhood in Indian society. Almost all Indian communities have a celebration before the baby is born where the mother-to-be is the centre of all the adulation.

The commercial produced in 1995 featured a mother-to-be and the family celebrating the forthcoming birth of the child. Again the film used a jingle format based on the evergreen 'Marriage' tune. In the film, Godrej Storwel is shown as an integral part of the family, being used for the safe-keeping of all family heirlooms and valuables —just as the mother-to-be is carrying the valuable heir-to-be!

Godrej Storwel Now

The revival of the sentimental hook for attracting the consumer had a role in strengthening Storwel's loyalty with its consumer. The brand continues to be the undisputed market leader. Even with a strong attack from Allwyn which offers a different, more modern looking product, Godrej has reigned supreme.

The Godrej Storwel advertising has helped the brand find a permanent place in the consumers' homes and minds. It is a shining example of how a rational offering (of a better product) can be significantly strengthened with the support of an emotional hook.

Creative

Given the strong appeal of the 'Marriage' commercial, it was decided to take cues from the film and piggyback on its memorability and likeability. A music track similar to the one used in the 'Marriage' film was used due to the former's high recall. It was decided to depict a middle class family situation which would cut across all regional barriers, just as the 'Marriage' commercial did. The situation was chosen after checking prevailing sentiments across all communities. The film featured a mother-to-be and the family celebrating the forthcoming birth of a child. The Godrej Storwel was shown as an integral part of the family, being used for the safekeeping of family heirlooms and valuables. The setting was 'Indian' and had a touch of the upper middle class for empathy.

Media

The media employed for the new communication was primarily TV supported by point of purchase publicity (POP) for in-store display in showrooms. Instead of a constant presence on TV, a "pulsing" strategy was employed with intense bursts to ensure top of the mind (TOM) presence, apart from advertising during the marriage and festival seasons. In addition, special consumer promotions were run periodically.

Godrej Storwel Today

Godrej Storwel continues to remain the image leader and retains its position as the largest selling brand of steel cupboards in the country today with a market share of five per cent. In fact, so strong is the brand position that a consumer buying a competitive cupboard asks for a Godrej even through what he is getting is not a Godrej Storwel. On the production front, it has upped its production capacity to meet the increased demand and reduce the time lag between order booking and delivery schedules.

The success of Godrej Storwel is an example of how a quality premium priced product can become a market leader and even become generic to the category, given an established distribution network and more importantly, advertising support that is original and relevant to the consumers' needs.

Godrej Storwel: Brand Building Tips

Consumer durable brands often need to justify a hefty premium (especially if competition is from the 'grey, unorganised' sector). It is often worth examining emotional issues, like Godrej Storwel, to justify the premium, rather than mere features and ingredients. Building a strong emotional bond with the consumers is the ultimate insurance against attack from low priced competition.

Godrej Storwel–Newly Married Couple

Film opens on a newly married couple entering home.
Sound Effects: Music

Cut to close-up bride setting her foot in her husband's house. The first step on the beloved's threshold.

Cut to the couple looking at the keys.
Sound Effects: Music

Cut to close-up of bride.
Sound Effects: Music

Cut to mom-in-law handing over a gift pack to the bride.
Jingle continues: May your life bloom like a garden of flowers....

Cut to the couple keeping their things in the Godrej Storwel.
Jingle: Now let's create more space.

Cut to dad and mom-in-law welcoming the couple.
Sound Effects: Music

Cut to close-up of a pair of keys in the gift pack.
Jingle continues: ... Let's start a new world together.

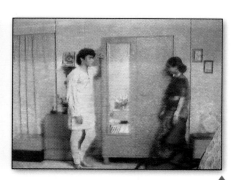

Film ends with close-up of Godrej Storwel and the husband and the wife standing on either side.
Jingle: Godrej Storwel.

Godrej Storwel—Pregnant Woman

Film opens on the grand-mom holding her ears to the pregnant woman's stomach.
Sound Effects: Music

Cut to mom-in-law hugging the pregnant woman.
Sound Effects: Music

Cut to the lady now removing her nose ring.
Jingle: Let's string the happiness together.

Cut to a lady welcoming the pregnant lady.
Jingle starts: My heart is singing.

The family playing around a boy who is sitting on top of a toy horse.
Jingle: The dad will play like a horse for the little one...

Cut to the lady standing near Godrej Storwel.
Jingle continues: And shower them on the little one.

Cut to the pregnant woman wearing a nose ring.
Jingle continues: ... and dancing with joy.

Cut to Grandma who is also dancing now.
Jingle:... Grandma will shower the little one with her blessings.

Film ends with close-up of Godrej Storwel and the couple standing near it.
Jingle: Storwel. Godrej Storwel.

Press Ad
Godrej Storwel
"Why spend time, money and effort..."

Press Ad
Godrej Storwel
"There's a lot more to a ..."

Press Ad
Godrej Storwel
"Why spend time, money and effort..."

Press Ad
Godrej Storwel
"My Only Choice..."

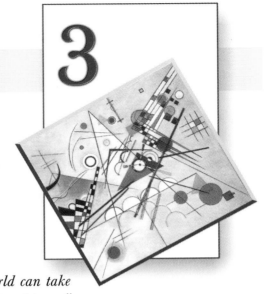

SECTION

Brand Building Services Advertising

"Press on. Nothing in the world can take the place of persistence."
• **Ray Kroc, McDonald's**

"There is only one boss. The customer. And he fires everybody in the company from chairman downwards, simply by spending his money somewhere else."
• **Sam Walton, Wal-Mart**

Credit cards, telecom services, airlines, housing loans, hotels—all offer services to customers and satisfy consumer needs in different ways. They are classified neither as consumer products nor as consumer durables. Hence a convenient sub-group name is given to them: services.

SERVICES

How do you define a service? Is it something you don't touch and feel? Is it something that is there yet not there?

With product parity being the rule of the day in consumer products and consumer durables, all products, in a way, are 'services' brands. Today, a number of products are positioned on the better services platform. But here we are not looking at them. We are looking at 'services' brands.

When we say 'services' brands, what comes to mind? Nothing. Don't be surprised. Services are probably the least 'branded' products, even in the global arena, where mega-services brands like AT&T and Sheraton exist.

What services brands can one think of in the Indian context?

Airlines	:	Indian Airlines, Jet Airways
Credit Cards	:	Citibank, Standard Chartered, ANZ Grindlays, HSBC
Telecom	:	MTNL, BPL, Escotel, Max Touch
Housing Loans	:	HDFC, CitiHome, LIC Housing
Television	:	Doordarshan, Zee
Hotels	:	Taj, Oberoi
Financial Institutions	:	ICICI, IDBI, SBI

And many more.

Unlike consumer products or consumer durables, none of these brands can be touched or held in our hands. So how does branding work?

Our old equation

$$\boxed{\textbf{Brand = Product + Image}}$$

Becomes

$$\boxed{\textbf{Brand = Services Received + Image}}$$

It is important to note that every time a consumer interacts with a service brand, it will change perceptions in some way. Unlike consumer products and consumer durables, every single interaction may be different. How often have we heard comments like:

"Last time I got much better service at this hotel."

So most services brands are focused at the first level to offer the same quality of services whenever a customer interacts with it. This in itself is a great achievement and builds the foundation for an image-building effort.

How does advertising work?

In the FCB grid examined earlier, services will feature across many quadrants:

Low Involvement Feeling	:	Television Channel?
Low Involvement Thinking	:	Cellular Service?
High Involvement Thinking	:	Credit Cards?
High Involvement Feeling	:	Hotel?

Advertising efforts in services are aimed not just at creating an 'image'. They often extend beyond image creation to soliciting a response, a visit, an enquiry.

In services advertising, it is often also necessary to consider all the various players who go on to build the brand—this may include, in the case of a tourist hotel—brand agents, town guides, hotel staff, food and beverage (F) & (B) staff etc.

Some of the most successful services brand advertising campaigns have worked first on the company staff. This is almost a litmus test on the effectiveness of such advertising.

Brand Building Advertising

Brand building advertising for services brands is faced with the challenge of appealing to various target groups, to create various responses. In fact, it is often necessary to fine-tune the objectives:

- Is advertising done to generate hard-leads?
- Is advertising done to generate positive associations?
- Is advertising aimed at building goodwill with associates etc.?

Given the fact that services brands present, virtually a different face every time a customer interacts with them, it is critical to ensure that the brand advertising always presents the same face. No wonder that some of the most standardised–formatted advertising is done in the hotel and airline industries! Who can forget the 'German' look of Lufthansa advertising, or the softer 'British-world' look of British Airways advertising?

At the next level is services brand advertising, which is task-driven. It is always a challenge to create a response-driven ad while staying tuned to the brand look and feel.

Lastly, advertising is often used to build a relationship with customers, agents and other associates. This, too, is a part of the brand building efforts for a services brand.

Services Brand Interactions

CASES

This section consists of cases in services brands, covering telecom, housing loans, financial services and tourism. As can be expected, these cases present a diverse range of tasks performed by services brand advertising. In that sense, they may not be 'brand' focused. But seen in the wider context, these advertising efforts too were geared towards building these brands, in "oh so many different ways"!

ESCOTEL—Branding a New Service

Company Background

Escotel Mobile Communications Ltd., a 51:49 joint venture between Escorts Limited and First Pacific Co. Ltd., was set up with the express purpose of spearheading Escorts' foray into the telecom sector.

Escorts is the flagship company of the Rs 3,400 crore Escorts Group, with diversified business in agr machinery, two-wheelers, construction equipment, automotive and railway ancillaries, financial services and telecommunication equipment and services.

First Pacific is an Asian conglomerate with interests in banking, marketing, real estate and telecommunications. It operates in 18 countries and had a turnover of US $ 8.3 billion in 1997. It was the first to introduce digital cellular technology in Hong Kong and operates the largest and fastest growing cellular service in the Philippines.

While Escorts had invested in the telecommunication services area earlier, its entry into the cellular phone service was expected to provide the front end and possibly the greatest opportunities in the telecommunication industry, which the company was keen not to miss out on.

The Markets

In May 1994, after the delicencing of the telecom sector, the country was divided into a number of cellular circles, with each circle being given to two service operators. Escotel won the bid for Haryana, Kerala and Uttar Pradesh (UP) (west) operations.

India was a nascent market for cellular telephony, and the consumer was not yet aware of its benefits. Therefore, there was a clear need for educating the target audience through concept selling of the generic benefits of cellular phones, to begin with. Only then was the task of creating brand differentiation by building one's own brand to be approached.

For Escotel, before it ventured forth with any marketing or communication plan, it was important to discern the fact that its market was not a homogeneous mass. The North-South divide was a reality. If for the north UP-ite or Haryanvi, business was all-important and making money was everything, the Keralite considered business important without being excessively materialistic. If the former was a social animal, the latter was a family man. And if the former had overt status needs, the latter was driven by a subtler need for status and a much greater rational sense.

The North-South Divide—Values and Lifestyles	
North	**South**
Business All-Important	Business Important
Material Wealth is Everything	Excessive Materialism is Bad
Have it. Flaunt it.	Have it. Keep it hidden away.
Social Animal	Family Man
Status is Everything	Respect is Everything
Emotional Animal?	Rational Animal?
(Two Stereotypes of Businessmen)	

Escotel was also confronted with the fact that there were few, if any, relevant conclusions one could draw from the experience of the cellular operators in the metros. Marketing a revolutionary new concept to upcountry markets was a very different kind of a challenge.

The Competition

In the three circles, competition came from:

    Kerala   – BPL (a strong national brand)
    U.P. (West)   – Koshika (street-smart operators)
    Haryana   – Essar (part of the largest national network)

Competitive Positioning

BPL – Headquartered in the south, it was a household name due to its presence in the brown and white goods markets. Collaboration with US West for cellular service operations. Had a 'son-of-the-soil' approach, aiming to encash its tremendous equity.

Koshika – Operated under the brand name 'Ushafone'. It was a price warrior which believed in building a consumer base by constantly dropping tariffs.

INFOLINE

WOMAN OF INDIA

Indian woman. Worshipped. Revered. Beaten up. Burnt. A spectrum of emotions.

Across India, the treatment of women varies. From urban to rural areas. From upper income households to lower income households. Even in urban India, it varies from big towns to small towns.

Amongst all this a trend is emerging. Indian women are becoming more and more assertive. They are joining the workforces in larger and larger numbers.

What are the stereotypes that are emerging?

Studies among women have sub-divided the two broad categories of Housewife and Working Women into further sub-categories. Among housewives we have categories like contemporary housewife, archetypal provider, troubled homebody etc. Among working women again there are differences, in their attitudes to work, family, children.

The exposure of all Indian women to television has had a role to play in their changing attitudes towards life. Many see a different life for their children and almost live their life through their children. Many move towards the setting up of nuclear households by cajoling, and coaxing their better halves.

But has the woman's lot really improved over the last 50 years in Independent India ? Have they become more vociferous? More demanding ? The picture is far from clear. However, today we don't have one stereotype, we probably have five!

Source: Business World
January, 8-12 1997

Essar — Sought to exploit its success in Delhi and the fact that it was the largest network in the country, to the maximum. Also Haryana being contiguous with Delhi gave them easier control and wider roaming benefits.

Escotel's Consumer Profile and Positioning

Research done by the agency threw up two key issues relevant to the task of positioning. These were:

- If the psychographic profile of the target person and his motivations varied a great deal between the north and the south, is there a case for positioning the service differently in the two places?
- Considering the fact that during concept testing, the slogan "Escotel keeps you ahead in business" was preferred over others, should we not position the brand as such rather than try to appeal to a wider base?

Intensive deliberations led to both the client and agency agreeing not to read literally into the research insights but to discern the nuances. It was strongly felt that while the consumer was different across the north and south with respect to his attitude towards life, family, society etc., his attitude towards cellular phones was quite similar. As regards the second point, it was felt that while eventually it would be business people who would represent the core target audience, at the outset, it would be better to keep the concept open and have an all-encompassing appeal. Given the limited understanding that people then had of the concept, it did not seem like a good idea to restrict oneself and talk only to business people.

In our markets, a key barrier to an individual's growth, success and prosperity was the abysmal quality of infrastructure, such as roads and communication systems. Years of dependence on and frustration with the inefficient and unreliable telephone department was not only an irritant, but a major obstacle to growth.

It was evident that a meaningful positioning would encompass a wider concept—a concept that had universal appeal and the promise of a different, better way of living. From this emerged the *positioning of 'Escotel Sansar'—a world of freedom, opportunities and prosperity which would welcome anyone with wide open arms.*

Role of Advertising

Given the nature of the product, its position in the lifecycle, and the peculiarities of our diverse markets, communication had to work at a number of levels. It needed to establish a strong brand identity for Escotel. It also needed to create an awareness of the cellphone concept and link it to the people's latent need to stay connected. And finally it needed to create a distinct brand differential, in order to develop consumer preference for Escotel.

Levels at Which Advertising Had to Work

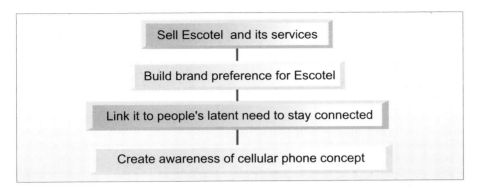

ADVERTISING STRATEGY

Phase I: Concept Selling

Since it was the first in the business in its circles, Escotel had not only the task of concept selling but also the opportunity of ascribing the generic benefits of cellular telephony to itself before the competition moved in.

The idea was to communicate the world of Escotel (Escotel Sansar), by creating vivid and identifiable images of happiness, prosperity and nearness.

In this scheme of things, the cellphone was used not as a status symbol, but as a device which would open new doors of opportunity even as it kept you connected with your near and dear ones.

> ### They Said So
>
> *"Advertising is salesmanship. Its principles are the principles of salesmanship. Successes and failures in both lines are due to like causes. Thus every advertising question should be answered by the salesman's standards."*
>
> • **Claude Hopkins**,
> *"Scientific Advertising"*

Phase II: Creating Differentiation

This was to be followed by a move towards a competitive pitch vis-à-vis the competitors. Here, unlike in the theme advertising, concrete Escotel advantages were identified, specific to each state.

The advantages were:

Kerala	– Microwave link transmission of Escotel offering the customers all-weather	vs. Land line transmission dependency of BPL

	and crystal clear communication. (state-of-the-art)		
Haryana	– Advantage of being the first in the market supplemented by microwave link technology	vs.	Late entry of Essar in spite of being contiguous to Delhi
U.P. (West)	– The widest coverage in U.P.(West) offered by Escotel along with quality service at reasonable rates.		Upstarts like Koshika who keep resorting to price drops for luring customers.

The underlying thought in this 'differentiator campaign' was that 'Escotel is simply the better choice'. This thought was to be drilled into the customer's mind with the rational supports mentioned.

Phase III: Tactical ads

This ran parallel with the differentiator advertising and comprised service launch ads (in different towns and cities of the three circles) and scheme ads such as those on handset bundling (special time bound offers on the cost of handset), free airtime, general announcements, festival greetings etc.

The brand was supported by other 'feel-good' activities like a starter's kit. This was fashioned as 'the Passport to Escotel Sansar' and was given to all subscribers, adding to the status implications.

Service Launches

Between November 1996 and January 1997, Escotel had launched its services in the following markets:

Haryana – Sonepat, Panipat, Karnal, Ambala, Panchkula, Yamunanagar.
UP (West) – Meerut, Agra, Aligarh.
Kerala – Ernakulam, Kozhikode, Thiruvananthapuram, Thrissur.

This made Escotel the first service operator to launch its services in almost all the above mentioned cities.

Press Ad
Escotel Cellular Phone Service
"New Freedom. New Togetherness..."

Press Ad
Escotel Cellular Phone Service
"New Confidence. New Success..."

Press Ad
Escotel Cellular Phone Service
"New Freedom. New Togetherness..."

Press Ad
Escotel Cellular Phone Service
"New Confidence. New Success.."

Press Ad
Escotel Cellular Phone Service
"New Freedom. New Horizons..."

Press Ad
Escotel Cellular Phone Service
"New Accessibility. New Hopes...."

THE RESULT

By the end of three months, as per market estimates, bookings stood as follows:

Circle	Escotel	Competition
Haryana	2,500	1,500
UP (West)	6,500	2,000
Kerala	3,300	2,000

This made Escotel not only the first service operator in each of its three circles, but also carried it significantly ahead of its competitors in the crucial first few months of the launch.

Escotel has continued to stay ahead of its competition, aided by an excellent service network and focused communication.

As on December 1998, the market share of Escotel in three circles is as follows:

Circle	Escotel	Competitor
Haryana	72%	28%
UP (West)	59%	41%
Kerala	65%	35%

Escotel's launch advertising built a strong foundation for the brand, across the country, in two diverse markets, by focusing on one key player in the services marketing game, the customer.

Escotel: Brand Building Tips

While selling a new 'high-tech' service, it is worth going beyond just jargon and generic selling. By creating a strong consumer focus in its communication, Escotel managed to build a service brand in a relatively short period.

HDFC—Building Affinity with a Key Intermediary

Background

The Housing Development Finance Corporation (HDFC), was set up in the 1970s with the explicit purpose of providing easy, affordable loans to the middle class households, for buying their own homes. HDFC has built its brand with its home loan customers through provision of easy procedures, courteous staff, excellent background work and reasonably attractive rates of interest.

HDFC, during its initial years, was aided by subsidised funds that it had received from international sources. This, coupled with a thoroughly professional approach to home loans, made HDFC almost a generic brand by the late 1980s.

In the 1990s, HDFC was faced with a new challenge. It had to source its funds from the local market for which it had to explore various avenues.

HDFC discovered that it enjoyed tremendous equity with the burgeoning middle class. Almost everyone knew someone who had had a good experience with HDFC, a great brand equity that could be used for mobilising funds.

HDFC went in for collecting fixed deposits (FDs) from retail investors. These deposits were of different types—non-cumulative/cumulative, one year/two years/three years etc. While HDFC did not offer interest rates similar to aggressive Non-Banking Financial Corporations (NBFC), it still managed to garner huge deposits, thanks to its image of trust, stability and safety.

Fixed Deposit Customer

India is probably one of the largest nations of moneysavers, with over 25 per cent of its GDP put aside for a rainy day.

Where do all the savings go?

Indians have a variety of saving options ranging from letting the money lie in a savings bank account to lending it at a (risky) high rate in the speculative market.

Savings: Risk vs Returns

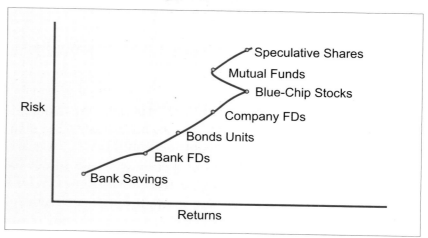

The Indian middle class was swinging wildly in the 1980s and the 1990s, across a wide spectrum of saving options. At one stage, large funds were flowing into shares and stocks, but this love affair crashed with the collapse/s of the market. Then came the affair with high-interest fixed deposits with speculative companies and plantation companies. This led to huge losses for the already battered middle class.

With all this happening in a relatively short period of 10 years, the middle class almost went into a shell. The NBFCs were seen as suspect, shares as speculative, and mutual funds as even more speculative.

The retail investor preferred to keep his money in low yielding bank deposits or in blue-chip NBFC deposits or bonds issued by large financial institutions like the IDBI.

HDFC benefitted from this trend. Its deposit products were seen as a source of very safe and medium returns. HDFC wanted to explore ways of building this equity and to look at innovative approaches to do so.

Customer—Brand Interface

Across the country, savings products like units, bonds, fixed deposits are marketed through 'agents' or 'brokers'. At the last count there were probably over 5,00,000 such agents across the country. All these agents market a whole bundle of products ranging from Life Insurance, PPF (Public Provident Fund), Units, Bonds/Debentures, Fixed Deposits and, at times, IPOs (Initial Public Offering of shares).

Many agents have a core group of customers who buy these products from them. Most of them operate out of their homes and often have a

MIDDLE CLASS MYTH

960 million people. The planet's largest democracy. Its second largest potential consumer market.

But how big is the market? 200 million? 100 million? 150 million?

A country of 960 million, over 160 million households. Less than 2 million tax payers? Over 40 million households with TV sets?

Indian's value perceptions change with the type of product they are looking at. So how does one define the middle class?

Is the middle class the target for cornflakes? If so, what is the target number?

Is the middle class the target for television? If so, what is the target number?

Sociologists believe Indians are highly value-driven with almost nothing going as waste. Newspapers get recycled. Clothes get handed down. TVs get reconditioned.

Hence, Indians are wary of expensive consumer items like cornflakes and cosmetics. However, if an Indian consumer perceives value, he will upgrade to a colour TV, a bigger refrigerator. In his mind, these are seen as 'investments' and not as consumption expenses.

Now with the real prices of durables dropping and resale values decreasing, will their perception of durables change in the future? It is difficult to say.

Source: Fortune, September 8, 1997
The Week, June 25, 1995

'regular' source of income as well. The agent is at times an extended family member who is invited for family functions and is treated with respect.

But why?

We, Indians, treat money with respect, and as an embodiment of the goddess 'Lakshmi'. Parting with money is often a carefully thought-out process and whoever we give our money to is seen as a person to be respected.

Most middle class householders are quite clueless about the nuances of various saving options. These are further complicated by un-friendly forms and procedures. Therefore, the agent is seen as a friendly adviser who can actually give unbiased advice to the head of the household on where to put the money.

As in the international markets, the first company to exploit the power of these agents was the Life Insurance Corporation of India (LIC). LIC had created a vast network of agents and kept them informed with various useful tips on how to sell insurance. Given the fact that LIC is for life, and the agents' commission is also for life, almost all agents market the LIC product. LIC, on its part, had rewarded this loyalty to offer various recognition devices to agents, like the Governors club etc.

Agent's Role Expanded

Agent	Householder
Advice of what investment? How much? In whose name? For what period? What are the old investments? When do they mature? Roll over?	I have so much to invest

Opportunity HDFC

HDFC realised that if it can create a positive bias in the minds of its agents, create a 'brand preference', it will pay back many times over. But isn't it too difficult? Too expensive?

HDFC was selling a me-too product and the interest rates it offered to the retail investors were not the most attractive. The brand, however, enjoyed a very good awareness and image with the investor. So if the agent was made to present the FD form to the customer it would do the trick, felt the company.

HDFC put down as its agenda to build–strengthen its relationship with its agents.

To this effect, FCB-Ulka Direct, the Direct Marketing Division of FCB-Ulka, was called in to devise a strategy to build a relationship with the agents.

HDFC Agents

The FCB-Ulka Direct team started analysing the agent base of HDFC, including having one-to-one interviews with key HDFC managers/ executives, high-performing HDFC agents, branch offices etc.

The verdict was unanimous. Agents thought very highly of HDFC. The company listened to them and was responsive to their needs. They had experienced no delays whatsoever in receiving their commissions, a common problem with many other corporates.

It was found that HDFC had, on its rolls, about 46,000 agents. To enable quick payment of commissions, the agents were dealt with on a day-to-day basis by the branch offices. This meant that the central marketing office was aware of only the names of the agents. It had no idea about how each agent performed, has growth etc.

HDFC Agents Relationship Programme

It was felt that the time was right to set up a relationship programme with HDFC agents. The objective: *To make the agent feel a bit closer to the brand HDFC.*

Heard-in-the-Agency

(Amusing exchanges between 'anxious' servicing and even more 'anxious' creative folks.)

"The client complimented you

on the _amazing_ execution

of such a powerful visual concept.

He _just_ wants to see it in

and a _single page_ format."

Step I: The Census

The agency, after talking one-to-one with a few agents, felt that the time was right to collect more detailed information from the 46,000 odd agents. It was felt that a number of them may be non-performing, while a number would be worth their weight in gold.

The agency devised an elaborate Census questionnaire form that was distributed to all the agents. The questionnaire sought information on the agents' total fund mobilisation capacity, key products' marketeers (LIC, Units, FDs, Bonds, PPF), growth/performance across products, the infrastructure offered, special services offered to customers, family details, future plans, ratings of HDFC etc.

• A Section of the Census Questionnaire

The Census questionnaire was sent out to all the 46,000 agents across the country. The questionnaire was accompanied with a detailed letter giving the agent the reason for the information collection. While there were doubts as to whether agents would reveal information about their collection of competitive products, it was felt that even if some of them gave that information it would add to the quality of data collected.

HDFC's branch offices were used to administer the questionnaire and the exercise received whole-hearted support from all the HDFC executives, across the country, (another key need when service brands are marketed).

Step II: Data Analysis

Completed questionnaires were received from over 25,000 Agents and every questionnaire unfolded a wealth of information.

On the basis of the data collected, HDFC could create a map of its agent field force:

- How many are fully active?
- How much are they collecting for HDFC?
- How much are they collecting as FD products?
- What are their past and future growth trends?
- What other services do they offer?
- What are their future plans?

All the information was fed into the agency's computer systems and data analysis commenced in full earnest.

Some interesting insights emerged:

- Just 10,000 agents mattered, they were the key as they held a huge potential!
- Agents rated HDFC very highly and welcomed the census survey!
- Agents looked forward to help from HDFC to improve their business!
- Almost all agents operated in their own names as well as those of family members!
- All agents wanted to expand their customer base, computerise, provide better services to customers!

And more!

Step III: HDFC Key Partners Programme

HDFC decided to create a 'key partner's programme' and enroll the top 10,000 agents. They were told that the club would provide them with useful information and value-added services, over a period of time.

The programme was launched with a newsletter titled "In-touch", which went out to all the selected members.

The newsletter was soon followed by a handy booklet on "How to sell an FD in HDFC" to a prospective customer. This booklet explained in a simple Question and Answer (Q&A) form how to explain the risk vs. return equation for HDFC vs. a smaller NBFC FD.

The objective of the programme was to provide the agents with value additions once in 3-4 months. To that extent, it was much more than just a newsletter programme.

Step IV: Value Additions

The Indian Government changed its rules regarding taxation and related matters in the year 1997, and this led to a lot of confusion, especially in the Agent community. All the HDFC key partner members received a handy compendium explaining the nuances of the new government policy to them in layman's language.

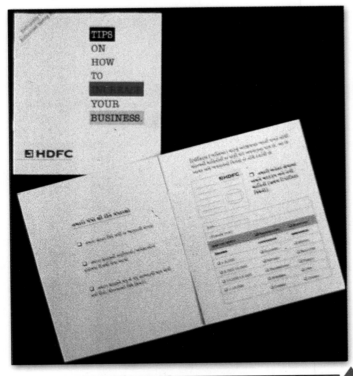

Direct Mailer
Housing Development Finance Corporation. Relationship Programme
"Tips on how to...."

Direct Mailer
Housing Development Finance Corporation. Relationship Programme
"An exclusive offer..."

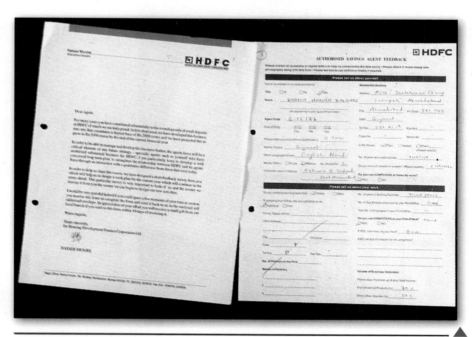

Direct Mailer
Housing Development Finance Corporation. Relationship Programme

Press Ad
Housing Development Finance Corporation. Relationship Programme
"Nice and Warm"

This was followed by an interesting tie-in offer. Just around 1997, pager companies were facing a glut. They had very few takers. HDFC tied up with one such company and offered a 'free pager' offer. HDFC provided the guarantee to the pager company, which in turn, waived off the signing-on fee and gave away the numeric pager free. While some agents took up the offer, the message well-received by all of them was "HDFC cares for us".

The Census survey had revealed that a large number of agents were planning to computerise. This led to the next tie-in offer. HDFC tied up with Aptech to offer special schemes for computer training. The Agent could walk in to his nearest Aptech Training Centre (with over 500 across the country, he was never far from one), and claim a special package on computer training.

Again a win-win-win situation, for HDFC, Aptech, and the agent.

These 'value additions' brought alive the concept that HDFC's key partners, its agents were, indeed, valued associates of HDFC.

THE RESULT

The programme, while it ran, was appreciated by all the agents. Every offer elicited numerous 'Thank you' letters. With no other FD marketing organisation running a relationship programme aimed at agents, HDFC's programme was the talking point at agent meets!

The programme helped glue the key intermediary, the agent to the brand, HDFC. The programme paid for itself many times over with increased collection, increased loyalty and increased brand imagery.

Ultimately building a services brand involves a lot more than just running a multi-media campaign. HDFC's agents relationship Programme, without the help of large budgets or heavy investments, added to HDFC's image as a brand that cares for its stake-holders!

HDFC Programme: Brand Building Tips

Service brands often neglect the intermediaries who can play a critical role in consumer brand choice. HDFC's agent Relationship Programme effectively demonstrates how it is possible to gain higher loyalty from intermediaries through focused efforts, that need not be highly expensive or time-consuming!

CASE STUDY

COCHIN EXPORT PROCESSING ZONE—Selling a Zone

BACKGROUND

The concept of an Export Processing Zone (EPZ) or Free Trade Zone was started way back in 1965 with the establishment of the Kandla Free Trade Zone. In 1974, in order to take advantage of the growing market for electronics and to ensure the transfer of latest technology to India, the Santacruz Electronic EPZ was started. With the growth in industrialisation, there was a need for more zones of this nature. As a result, the Government established more EPZs in Madras, Cochin and Noida in the early 1980s. These free trade zones were established with the objective of boosting exports, encouraging foreign investment, providing more employment and helping create a strong technological base by encouraging the transfer of the latest technology.

COCHIN EXPORT PROCESSING ZONE (CEPZ)

This zone was started in 1986 as a tax-free industrial zone, which formed an enclave within the national customs territory. It was conceived and established keeping in mind Cochin's intrinsic strengths as a global business centre. CEPZ is strategically located on India's south-west coast. The CEPZ offered plots and services to set up 100 per cent export units and allowed 25 per cent of the production to be sold in India. CEPZ provided a tax-free zone with benefits such as exemptions from income tax, sales, excise duty and customs duties.

Competition

The labour situation in Kerala has always looked grim to anyone who is entering the market for the first time. Strikes occuring at the drop of a hat, production closing down, massive financial losses etc. seem to dog the heels of any new entrepreneur who has not understood the puzzle that is Kerala. Hence, the entrepreneurs have always been mighty cautious about entering into this particular market. One of the first problems that CEPZ had to tackle was this negative perception about the labour in Kerala.

WRITING BETTER CREATIVE BRIEFS

How to prepare a brief? A good brief should work on a number of levels. It tells creative people what the advertising task is and what we are asking them to fulfil. It also gives creative people an understanding and insight into the brand and the advertising target.

The brief should be exactly that. Brief. However, there are some guidelines, and these are set.

Objective

- This is the objective of this piece of work.
- It may vary from the advertising objective of the company as described in the strategy. If it does, make it brief and specific.

Consumer Benefit

- The promise, the USP or the unique selling proposition.
- This is the single benefit which distances this product or service from the competition.
- The promise must be strong and simple.
- Remember to translate a product benefit into a consumer benefit.

Support

- List all the relevant facts that lead you to the single product benefit.
- Remember only the relevant facts.

Tone and Manner

- This is the personality of the brand speaking. It must have a definite character.
- Products, like people, must have definite, memorable, unique personalities if they are to become stars.

Mandatories

- These are only facts not opinions, not subjective views or traditional folklore.

Media Budget

- It is useful to know how much money is going to be put behind a particular campaign.

Production Budget

- Be specific and realistic—not miserly.
- If there's only a small budget, admit it.

Source: Ulka Datasite, 1996-97

In terms of competition, CEPZ had to contend with the special incentives for the new industries given by the government. This was because industrialisation had become a major priority area at that time for the government. Special incentives were being offered by the governments of various states, to promote investments in their respective states. This resulted in stiff competition in selling industrial land.

The Cochin Export Processing Zone faced competition from the other EPZs, who offered the same facilities as the CEPZ and from the State and Central Government industrial plots.

The Advertising Objective

The advertising objective for the agency when it acquired the account, was to attract 100 per cent export units to the zone and thereby sell its plots and services, and to attract foreign investments to the zone.

The Positioning

The agency conducted an exploratory study among the target group to decide on the positioning of the CEPZ. The positioning had to be done carefully since the agency was trying to sell a service. The entrepreneurs, who were the target segment identified by the agency, were looking for options where there would be availability of raw materials and manpower and proper infra-structural facilities. Also, they were looking at states where they would not have to waste time on unnecessary procedures. The entrepreneurs needed a place where they could put their units into pro-duction as soon as possible and for a place that could double up as a marketplace for their finished products.

> ### They said so
>
> *"People can be coaxed but not driven. Whatever they do, they do to please themselves. Many fewer mistakes would be made in advertising if these facts were never forgotten."*
>
> •**Claude Hopkins,**
> *"Scientific Advertising"*

The entrepreneurs were having a tough time keeping to their schedules due to the red tape they faced while setting up production units in other industrial estates. They were losing a lot of precious time on trying to work around the system. The agency decided that CEPZ should be positioned as a service that would fulfil all the entrepreneurs' demands and enable them to carry out their work on schedule. It had to have a strong impact on the person who saw it and had to be precise in its meaning. The positioning statement that was finally decided upon was *'Cochin Export Processing Zone'*

—The quickest route to exports'. The statement would spark an immediate response. The words, 'the quickest route to exports' tackled the problem uppermost in the entrepreneur's mind, that of keeping pace with the schedule.

The Creative

The creative was designed keeping in mind the fact that the decision-makers for the product would be busy executives who would not have time to go through an elaborate ad. The buying process would be a long drawn out one since lots of time would be needed to deliberate over the rationale behind buying a service like CEPZ.

The advertising strategy comprised press ads highlighting the CEPZ advantages and an information booklet on CEPZ. The strategy was to make the message brief but interesting in such a way, that it created immediate interest and quick responses. The strategy focused on the theme—the shortcut for exporters.

The press ads were designed for maximum noticeability and powerful impact. It had bold headlines to catch the immediate attention of the target audience. The ad copy was kept to the minimum and a reply coupon was introduced to elicit quick responses. In fact the coupon was the most important part of the ad layout–the hero in the ad. The headlines aimed to project CEPZ as a quick acting organisation, again reiterating the positioning. The phrase "quickest route to exports" was used as a baseline.

The body copy was kept to the minimum, keeping in mind the fact that the entrepreneurs would not have time to read through the entire information in one go. The function of the body copy was to elicit a quick response for the detailed information rather than to provide all the details in the ad itself. The coupon was aimed at people who wanted further details. This ensured that the people who answered the coupon would be people who were prospective customers. The coupon responses would help create a database for further use.

The booklet of information was the next step. This booklet would be sent in response to the coupons. The booklet had all the information required to set up a project in CEPZ along with the facilities and incentives that CEPZ offered. The advertising was intended to project CEPZ a quick-acting organisation, which offered comprehensive facilities for exporters.

The media objective was to create interest and generate requests for more information. The ads were placed in select newspapers and magazines, both Indian and foreign, aimed at catching the attention of the target group.

Press Ad
Cochin Export Processing Zone
"Take a holiday from income tax..."

Press Ad
Cochin Export Processing Zone
"Cut red tape..."

Press Ad
Cochin Export Processing Zone
"For Power, manpower and brainpower..."

RESULTS

This campaign pulled in over 6,000 responses asking for more information and formalities for setting up an export-oriented unit (EOU), in the zone. The database thus generated was followed up with direct selling activities, leading to a jump-start for CEPZ, overcoming the huge odds that the zone had faced.

The 'CEPZ' brand was thus established quickly in the target group's mind. Today CEPZ is a throbbing hive of activity–truly providing a shortcut for exporters.

> ## CEPZ: Brand Building Tips
>
> While selling complex brand offerings, to a select target audience, in a very high involvement category, the best way could be to get 'interested' customers to take 'action'. CEPZ achieved a dramatic response by playing up the 'coupon' and the 'call-for-action', instead of trying to 'sell' the entire service offering.

BANGARAM ISLANDS: Thank God for Nothing

The liberalisation of the Indian economy in the 1980s and the 1990s brought about many changes, at both the micro and macro levels. The rise in income levels, and increasing urbanisation have been coupled with higher standards of living and increased consumer aspirations. Almost overnight, the Indian consumer's lifestyle has undergone a transformation. He is willing to pay more, if he sees 'value' in the purchase. He is willing to pay for the best, if he thinks that's what he wants.

As the pace of life increased, the consumer was getting more and more squeezed for time, more importantly quality time. Leisure activities were at a premium and were much sought after by the consumer.

Till the 1980s holidays meant a trip to one's 'native' place to visit one's parents, cousins, grand parents et al. They expanded at times to planned trips to the holy cities but very rarely to include typical holiday destinations like Simla and Ooty—that too primarily for the upper classes.

With increased income levels, a transformation took place. The upper-upper classes set their eyes on international locations like London, Paris, New York. The middle classes or the upper middle classes now hankered after the Simlas and Goas. This wanderlust was tapped by a new service product, time-share holidays. Overnight marketeers of time-share holidays were falling all over each other to woo the upper middle class. In order to outdo each other, marketeers began offering the consumer greater options and wider choices—one year at Goa, the next at Kochi, the year after abroad and so on for 99 years, if this intense holidaying doesn't knock you out before then. (Well, the time-share bubble burst in the late 1990s.)

In this confusion was emerging a small group of 'quality' holiday makers, looking for a tranquil holiday location, a different experience, far from the madding crowd.

In the 1990s, the world started looking at India as a possible holiday destination. Agra-Jaipur-Goa started featuring in several tour guides. The more adventurous European traveller was looking beyond these destinations to Kerala, Tamil Nadu, Orissa, Rajasthan, Varanasi!

Holiday Ladder

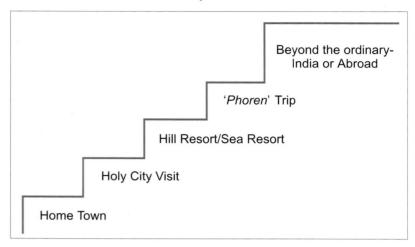

BANGARAM ISLANDS

Bangaram Islands is one of the 30 islands in Lakshadweep, a Union Territory of the Government of India. With 128 acres of uninhabited tropical land, vast stretches of beaches, lush vegetation, coral reefs and crystal clear water, it was really 'Paradise Regained'.

Casino Group is one of Kerala's leading business groups with interests in hotels, exports and travel services. In 1989, Casino Group took over Bangaram Islands for promoting it as an exotic tourist destination. Its beautiful beaches, coral reefs, crystal clear water made it ideal for activities like snorkelling, scuba diving and deep sea fishing.

Bangaram Islands was in many ways cut off from civilisation with no telephones, no TV, and no newspapers.

Casino Group decided to convert these into the virtues of the resort—the Bangaram Island Resort. 30 cottages were set up across the island, capable of accommodating 60 adults. It was decided that while electricity would be provided, the Resort would not have any other trappings of the civilised world.

Casino Group roped in FCB-Ulka to brainstorm on how to brand and market this unique property. It was clear from the beginning that this

PLANNING BETTER ADVERTISING STRATEGIES

What is strategy? Strategy is essentially a statement of what the advertising is trying to do. It is both the base on which advertising is developed and the action standard against which creative work will be judged.

How to Formulate a Strategy?

It requires a combination of careful, deductive thinking and imaginative flair. The planner not only needs to be able to see the wood from the trees, but also to think what the wood would become like if the trees were changed. The five parts of the written strategy have been detailed below:

Marketing Aims

- All marketing aims should adhere to the RUMBA principle. They must be relevant, understandable, measurable, believable and achievable (RUMBA).
- Check your aim against these five criteria before you continue.

Advertising Objectives

- Our advertising should communicate a specific message. Be realistic.
- Relate the objective to the budget. Again, apply the RUMBA principle.

Target Group

- Be specific but not over-precise.
- Try and build a character study of the potential consumer — the real person.

Competitive Frame

- This is a battle strategy.
- To win the battle, one must know the enemies and what their strategies are likely to be.
- You cannot over-research this section.
- Supply as much information as possible.
- The most essential part of this section is competitive advertising.
- Get a reel of every competitive commercial and copies of all their ads.

Consumer Perception

The key to this section is to remember that all our advertising has to do is prepare the consumer for that moment:

- Brand choice. We have to change his mind.
- How our target market consumer views us now and how we want our consumer to view us, after we have run the campaign.

Source: Ulka Datasite, 1996-97

would be a premium holiday destination, both for Indians and for foreign travellers. In addition to the room tariffs, the guest would spend a significant amount to reach the island. So it had to be the kind of tourist who had the money power and more importantly the 'attitude' and 'interest' in a 'typical' holiday, far away from civilisation.

Positioning Bangaram Islands

India boasts of numerous beach resorts like Goa, Kovalam, Gopalpur-on-sea. Many of them are popular destinations visited by international and Indian travellers. Bangaram had to offer something different.

It was decided that the resort would be the 'ultimate natural experience'. The positioning was brought alive by the USP offered —no TV, no airconditioner, no newspaper, only the sea, sea and more sea.

The positioning of Bangaram Island resort was not a statement, but was the resort itself!

Wooing Indian Tourists

It was felt that there existed a small, influential group of Indian holiday makers who might find Bangaram just perfect for an exotic holiday. But how big was this group? Was it worth concentrating only on this segment? FCB-Ulka was assigned the task of targeting these travellers on a small budget.

Heard-in-the-Agency

"You don't know how lucky you are that you're not an Account Executive. I've got to take this campaign out to the real world ... and sell it."

The agency felt that it was necessary to present the resort as the "last of the enchanted isles"–in all its glory. The resort had to appeal to the wanderlust of the upper-upper income group and the job had to be accomplished on a shoestring budget.

The agency decided to target the readers of India's leading business daily, 'The Economic Times.' A large colour ad appeared in the Friday colour section of 'The Economic Times' presenting Bangaram as "Thank God, for nothing". The ad offered interested readers further information in the form of a booklet or a VHS cassette (for a fee of Rs 100).

The single release created a deluge of enquiries leading to large bookings.

Bangaram had arrived on the upper-upper Indian's tourist map! The resort built up on this momentum and repeat customers as well as word-of-mouth referrals kept the resort buzzing with activity.

But Bangaram needed more.

Discerning International Travellers

Bangaram had to attract foreign travellers to meet its objective—foreign travellers could further be sold other holidays in and around Kerala, in properties owned by the Casino Group.

Bangaram focused its efforts on travel agents and tour operators in leading European countries. This was coupled with efforts focused on travel writers and holiday magazines. Selected travel agents and travel writers were brought to Bangaram to get a taste of the resort, first hand. This effort paid off in dollars, pounds and marks!

Bangaram started featuring as a premium exclusive travel spot for the really adventurous traveller!

Press Ad
Bangaram Islands
"Thank God, He Created Nothing"

RESULT

Bangaram is today an exclusive property, that is marketed almost entirely by word-of-mouth. The resort runs almost to full capacity during the season when it is open.

More importantly for the Casino Group, it is attracting the discerning sea-lover to Bangaram. (One story goes that Casino even paid back the booking amount to the family of an Indian businessman who demanded TV).

Casino Group is building on this learning curve by operating several such small but 'different', 'exclusive', properties across Kerala.

Bangaram Resorts: Brand Building Tips

Building a 'resort' brand calls for a total brand experience, starting with romantic advertising to the real experience at the resort. The Bangaram brand was built with a mixture of advertising, public relations, publicity and most importantly, the brand experience and WOM (word-of-mouth) of satisfied customers.

Brand Building Corporate Advertising

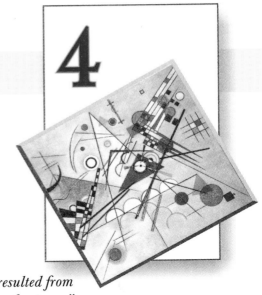

"The great accomplishments of man have resulted from the transmission of ideas and enthusiasm."

• **Thomas J. Watson Jr., IBM**

Corporate brands come in many sizes and shapes. They are as large and industrial as ABB or as small and intimate as Apple. While dealing with corporate brands, we run the entire gamut, from corporate brands that also act as consumer product brands to corporate brands that offer no product or service to the end-consumer.

CORPORATE BRAND

What is really a corporate brand? Is it just the corporation visualised as a brand? Or it is the range of products offered under a corporate brand name?

The area is vast, so one needs to tread a little carefully. It makes sense to look at some classic examples:

- Sony. It is a consumer durable brand. And a corporate brand.
- Coca Cola. It is a consumer product brand. And a corporate brand.
- 3M. It is a corporate brand. It offers many products under many brand names, and some under 3M.
- Thermax. It is a corporate brand. It offers heavy equipment under this brand name.
- Hindustan Lever Limited (HLL). It is a corporate brand. It offers virtually no product under this brand name.

So it is rather difficult to define where the line is to be drawn.

(A) Corporate brands are brands that offer products and services under that name. In such cases they are umbrella brands.

(B) Corporate brands are also names that offer no product or service under that name, except for share certificates. In such cases their range of appeal is narrower.

Brand Architecture Model

Corporate Brand	:	Hindustan Lever	Colgate-Palmolive
Product Brand	:	Lux	Palmolive
Line Brand	:	Lux International	Naturals
Variant Brand	:	Olive Enriched	Olive Enriched

A Corporate brand, be it in type A or type B, has a wide variety of target consumers to talk to. In the case of type A it includes consumers. In the case of type B, it is consumers like shareholders, suppliers, associates, employees, financial institutions, government bodies etc.

So a corporate branding programme needs to encompass a wider spectrum of the target audience, depending on the objective of the programme.

Corporate Brand's Net

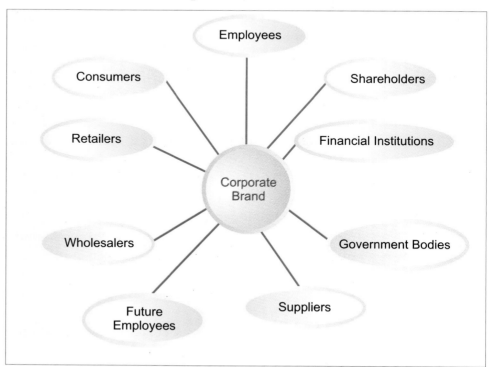

How Does Advertising Work?

Corporate brand advertising ranges from advertising aimed at selling a product/service carrying the brand name, to advertising aimed at mobilising funds in an IPO, to awareness building programmes before a new product/service is offered.

Corporate brands have first of all, to be seen as more than just:

- a product
- a service
- a factory
- an office
- a R&D establishment
- a team
- a share certificate

Corporate brands need to be seen as:

Brand = Corporate Offerings/Strengths + Image

The role of advertising in corporate brands depends on the offer. If the corporate brand is offering high value computers, one model will be used, if it is a low value supply, then a different model will be used.

For instance, the role of advertising will be different if it is:

- Thermax   –   selling boilers
- Tata Finance   –   selling truck loans
- Xerox   –   selling copies
- Wipro   –   selling bulbs

However, the principles of good advertising will apply: advertising will have to be based on a well thought out strategy and should be interesting, stimulating and likeable!

Brand Building Corporate Brand Advertising

It is difficult to look at corporate brand advertising as distinctly different from, say, a services brand or a high value durable brand. So for the sake of focus, let us examine only corporate brand building exercises that go beyond a product.

Brand building with respect to corporate brands per se extends beyond a product. It has to cover a wider target profile–employees, stockholders, suppliers etc. Given this wider gamut of target audience, it is often difficult to get to one specific target, and most corporate brand advertising ends up lacking focus.

So, it is imperative that the prime focus be defined clearly at the outset itself. It is better, then, to relegate all the other target segments as 'also rans'. In the case of IBM the target is always the prospective customer. In the case of British Petroleum, it is often opinion leaders/influencers. It is not that all other consumers, are unimportant, but quite simply the organisation believes it needs to give communication the focus.

After getting the focus, corporate brands need a positioning. Globally corporate brands are positioned on three broad planks:

- Innovation
- Value
- Customer Service

These broad platforms can further be sub-divided to give the corporate brand the required long term positioning statement.

Finally, like all brand building advertising, corporate brand building advertising will also have to be relevant, unique, believable and, above all, interesting. Even a boiler can be made to sound interesting for the person taking a decision to buy a boiler, it is indeed a very interesting product.

CASES

The following section consists of a collection of cases, spanning a variety of corporate brands. It may be argued that these cases could very well have been in a different section, but they have been grouped here more to give a feel for the diverse nature in which corporate brands are advertised.

WIPRO—We've been Thinking of You

Wipro is one of India's true success stories. A corporate with its roots in edible oils, it successfully diversified into soaps, computer hardware, computer software, healthcare systems, lighting products and financial services.

Wipro is among the top in every market it competes in and employs probably the best brains in the country in every sphere of its activity.

1997, THE NEW ERA

Wipro's business units are run as independent companies with independent marketing and brand communication resources. Given the intense individualism the company encourages, each unit marches to its own tune.

INFOLINE

PRESENTATION CHECKLIST

1. Presentation material (transparencies, slides, flip charts, film etc.) sequentially in order and preferably numbered or marked for identification. Also prepare a cue-sheet for the presentation.

2. Some blank transparencies with a set of OHP markers.

3. Overhead projector/slide projector with slide trays/TV–VCR etc., as required (please check in advance for working conditions and/or quality of projection/picture).

4. Extension cord and an adaptor.

5. Remote control units for each of the electronic items (if available).

6. An OHP pointer (if available), cello-tape and a few soft-board pins.

7. A few blank papers and paper clips.

8. Some writing pads and pencils for the audience at the present-ation.

9. The overall arrangements which include lighting, seats, refresh-ments, airconditioning/ventilations etc. in the presentation room.

Source: *Ulka Datasite*, 1996-97

An analysis of the business revealed that Wipro offered a number of products and services under the name Wipro:

- Wipro Super Genius PCs
- Wipro Software
- Wipro Soaps
- Wipro Lighting
- Wipro Services

Is there an opportunity to leverage these diverse skills into something that is bigger than the sum of its parts?

What is the real Wipro?

APPLYING THOUGHT

Wipro embarked on an extensive nationwide search to get to the heart of the Wipro brand with the help of the international Brand Consultant, S.R. Sengupta.

Extensive group discussions were held with consumers of various Wipro products and services like:

- Young mothers using Wipro baby soaps
- Buyers of Wipro Fixed Deposits
- Buyers of Wipro lighting products
- Buyers of Wipro software and services

Wipro decided that the brand needed a new look to reflect its changing ethos for the next millennium.

Wipro: Applying Thought

After extensive research, the rainbow flower design and the base line, 'Applying Thought' were finalised. The Wipro brand was to be customer–oriented offering its customers:

- Innovation
- Value for Money
- Customer Support
- Integrity

in every product and service it offered.

CORPORATE BRAND ADVERTISING

The new livery of Wipro brand was announced with fanfare through extensive public relations efforts covering the national press and TV media.

Wipro called in FCB-Ulka to devise a corporate brand ad campaign to present the new corporate look and the many faces of Wipro.

It was decided to focus efforts on five key areas of business:

- Computer Hardware
- Computer Software
- Computer Services
- Lighting Products
- Baby Products

These five areas of business were selected to present the wide range that Wipro offered and it was required to present each of these areas within the ambit of Wipro's core values of innovation, customer care, value and integrity.

What emerged was a six ad campaign that ran across national media, in newspapers and magazines. Research was again used extensively to fine tune the copy strategies and media strategies.

Heard-in-the-Agency

"The RESEARCH team feels that the ad tested _rather well_. They liked what the ad said. It's just that they could _not comprehend it._"

Press Ad
WIPRO
"You'll wonder what the Internet can..."

The more you care, the more attention you pay. That's how our R&D labs developed regular light bulbs that last 30% longer.

We've been thinking of you.

WIPRO
Applying Thought

Press Ad
WIPRO
"The more you care, the more attention you pay..."

You want the best for your little one. So we put milk and almonds into our baby soap, to care for her tender skin.

We've been thinking of you.

WIPRO
Applying Thought

Press Ad
WIPRO
"You want the best for your little one..."

BRAND BUILDING ADVERTISING ■

The first burst ran from August 1998 to November 1998.

Post-Test

Wipro had set up benchmarks comparing Wipro with key competitors in various segments of business including computers, lighting, baby products etc. The first benchmark study was done in August 1997. The study was repeated in November 1998, to gauge the impact of the entire communication programme.

Between August 1997 and November 1998, the consumer had been subjected to a lot. Three new Prime Ministers. Rapid increase in prices. Increased lawlessness. Infrastructure logjam. A drop in GDP growth.

Wipro had marginally improved its ratings between 1997 and 1998. So was the communication programme a failure? When scores were compared across other companies benchmarked, interesting lessons emerged. Almost every company that was benchmarked, in every segment, had dropped in image terms, while Wipro had held on and in some cases improved its ratings.

Wipro has managed to emerge as a new brand with its new identity, and new communication programme. The Wipro brand is today among the most salient and its future looks even brighter.

Wipro: Brand Building Tips

Corporate brands often straddle a variety of products and services. It is necessary to unify the offering with a common 'purpose'. Wipro achieved this with their 'Applying Thought' base line. The advertising then has to unify the offers in a 'one look' and 'one copy approach'. Wipro managed this with the "We've been thinking of you" line and each advertisement explaining how Wipro is 'Applying Thought' across various offerings.

CASE STUDY

TATA FINANCE—'Peace of Mind'

In the early 1980s the Indian economy was still to wake up to the liberalisation era. Laws and regulations tied numerous projects into inextricable knots. Taxation laws were tougher still. Indian business groups suddenly discovered the advantages of having their own finance companies. These subsidiaries gave them an option of borrowing money from the market, dabble in the stock market and in the process save a lot of money on taxation. A whole new breed of companies was born!

Almost every company got into the act and set up a finance company. How many would survive? How many would grow? How many would become institutions?

TATA FINANCE

Tata Finance Ltd. was set up in the early 1980s with the objective of becoming a financial institution, offering a wide range of services to investors, group companies and associates.

Tata Finance, built on the strong foundation of the Tata Group, grew slowly and steadily. While many other finance companies took the adventurous route, the risky route, Tata Finance played it by the rules, building its brand equity in the retail and the institutional markets.

FUND BASED AND NON-FUND BASED ACTIVITIES

A Non-Banking Financial Company (NBFC) basically 'buys' and 'sells' money and arranges for the 'purchase' and 'sale' of money.

'Fund based activities' are activities whereby the NBFC borrows money from the market by taking fixed deposits or cumulative deposits from retail investors. This class of investors are basically from the middle class, each of them putting their savings into the fixed deposits of NBFCs to earn an extra 4–5 per cent that is offered as opposed to the interest offered by banks. The NBFC then uses this money for fund based activities like hire-purchase and lease of assets. Here again the range is vast, starting from the hire-purchase of a durable, vehicle, commercial vehicle to the lease of assets like plant and machinery, for large companies.

Risk vs. Return

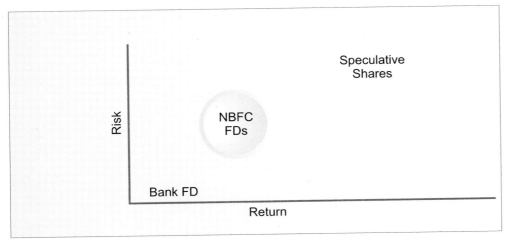

'Non-fund based activities' involve areas like loan syndication, merchant banking etc. wherein the NBFC is not funding the activity but is arranging for the fund, by acting as an intermediary. In these activities, NBFCs earn their income through a commission system unlike in the fund based activity where the difference in borrowing rate and lending rate, 'the spread', becomes the operating income for the NBFC.

With each corporate group vying for funds, the NBFCs started getting very aggressive in the market in the late 1980s. While the RBI controlled the interest rates, NBFCs found ways to circumvent these rules by offering 'incentives', over and above the interest rate allowed. In net effect, they were 'buying' money at an alarmingly high rate.

On the other side, NBFCs started aggressively 'selling' money, to their own group companies in the form of lease financing, as well as to retail customers, in the form of hire-purchase.

The market, in one word, was 'overheated'. Retail investors were demanding more and getting it. Hire-purchase customers were being wooed actively, with attractive offers.

Tata Finance Positioning

In this overheated market, Tata Finance decided to position itself as "the finance company from India's largest business house"–the Tata Group. The Tata Finance brand was to stand for stability and integrity. The focus was on providing steady, yet adequate returns and complete safety and security.

Tata Finance had decided to play it by the rule book—never to borrow or 'buy' at an unreasonable rate and never to 'sell' to a doubtful customer.

But was this possible in the prevailing market scenario? Tata Finance decided to strengthen certain areas of its operations to take on its aggressive rivals:

- Never compromise the Tata Finance name.
- Set up front-offices across the country—28 branches were set up—each reflecting the Tata Finance brand equity.
- Provide the best possible service to the retail customer.

INFOLINE

IDEATION

Where do those clever advertising guys get their ideas from? This question is often asked by the lay consumer. But is it an art, a science or a bit of both? Can it be taught or are you born with it?

Creativity or ideation in advertising is often the discovery of connecting unconnected objects. Men in towels to washing machine. Mistaken age to a soap.

There are regular methods used by experienced hands to develop ideas. Edward de Bono taught the world lateral thinking and in advertising, a number of teachers have expanded the arsenal of ideation techniques.

The simplest and the most often used ideation technique is random word association. Through this technique creative people in the agency attempt to link the problem at hand to an unconnected object. Voila an idea is born! The random word can be pulled out of a book, a magazine or even the dictionary.

The parallel to this is associating random pictures to a product-brand or problem at hand. Gymnastics—to a low fat breadspread. Cart wheeling kid—to a cooking oil.

It is always a challenge to get the right idea, that will lead to advertising that will be in tune with the strategy, that will sell the brand today and build brand values overtime.

Source: FCB-Ulka

This strategy of taking the Tata Finance name into the market paid off. Tata Finance became more visible and its name became synonymous with a solid-stable-reliable finance company.

The company felt that in order to grow in the long term, Tata Finance had to build its brand equity with its various target publics. There was a need to position Tata Finance, well away from all the other NBFCs in the market.

Issues Facing Tata Finance

Tata Finance stood for stability and reliability. However, in the NBFC market, it was not seen as a 'big' name. In fact, NBFCs like Sundaram Finance had a much bigger 'halo' in the market.

Tata Finance was perceived as a 'truck' finance company, or, at best, a company with a primary focus on financing 'Tata' products only.

Tata Finance was not seen, by the target consumers, as the most 'customer driven' NBFC. The communication had to add a strong dose of 'warmth' to the Tata Finance brand.

The FCB-Ulka team took the analysis further and discussed the issues with the Tata Finance team. The issues were further identified as specifics to be tackled. Tata Finance had to build its brand equity across various target customers:

- Fixed Deposit (FD) Customers
- Hire-Purchase Customers
- Institutional–Lease Customers
- Loan Syndication Customers

The range covered the entire spectrum from a retired schoolmaster in a small town (who is the FD target customer) to the Managing Director of a medium sized company in a metro city (who wanted Tata Finance to arrange for a bridge loan).

The primary target for the mass media communication was the FD customer. The others were more accessible through direct contacts, but the FD customer, scattered across the country, was seen as the key target.

The task with respect to the FD customer was seen as two-fold:

- Build Tata Finance awareness and image
- Convert the positive equity to FDs by positioning and selling the FDs 'differently'.

Tata Finance came out with a three ad (press) image-building campaign. The three ads spoke of three specific areas of activities of Tata Finance: hire-purchase, fixed deposits and loan syndication. The ads were released in colour and in large size in leading dailies and magazines, given the objective that Tata Finance had to be seen as:

- a large company
- a multi-dimensional company
- a progressive company

The campaign departed from the standard NBFC norm of just selling products/services and sold the Tata Finance name instead.

The campaign set the stage for the active marketing of Tata Finance FD.

Tata Finance FDs: Not just a deposit!

How does one sell a product that is really no different (in its basic features) from those offered by the competition?

Tata Finance FDs had to be positioned differently, not just on dimensions of safety or returns. It was felt that to the primary target consumers, the middle-aged, the middle class customers, the FD is a lot more than just a means of saving or an instrument. They expect the FD to come in handy in their time of need. They, in fact, see the FD as more than just a 'deposit'.

From this insight was born the tag line:

'Tata Finance Fixed Deposits. Not just an investment. A friend'.

How could one make the idea of a 'very safe' FD come alive in the consumers' mind? That was the thrust of the communication—the creative challenge.

NBFCs were coming under a cloud. A number of them shut shop, after duping thousands of investors. Even some of the 'banks' were being seen as unsafe!

What did Tata Finance FD offer in this scenario? The prime target investor was the middle class, middle-aged person. He/She knew that there were other better investment options–but they were not as 'safe'. Why would he invest in a Tata Finance FD? What was he looking for?

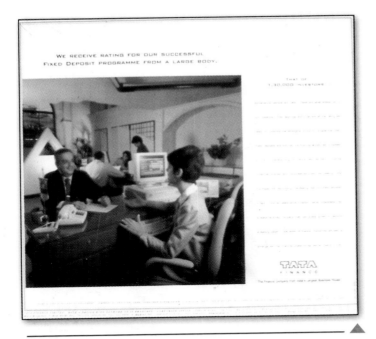

Press Ad
Tata Finance Ltd.
"We receive rating for our..."

Press Ad
Tata Finance Ltd.
"In one year, our disbursals..."

CHAPTER 4 ■ BRAND BUILDING CORPORATE ADVERTISING

Press Ad
Tata Finance Ltd.
"As a leading player in the short term..."

Press Ad
Tata Finance Ltd.
"Find Purpose. The Means Will Follow..."

BRAND BUILDING ADVERTISING ■

It was felt that Tata Finance, with its strong track record of being a safe—trust worthy investment option, spelt 'worry-free' investments for the investor.

From here was born the theme: "Peace of Mind!"

The press copy went on to say that Tata Finance fixed deposits have one key benefit (not offered by many others): Peace of Mind!

The theme, was carried through in all the elements of communication when interest rates went up the tactical ads said 15 per cent Interest. 100 per cent "Peace of Mind." The Theme "Peace of Mind" started by Tata Finance FD's has been much instated by a number of other campaigns including the campaign run by the government of India for Voluntary Disclosure of Income Scheme (VDIS).

Tata Finance FDs: The Growth

The concerted brand building campaign in media, the front-office strategy, the well motivated selling team and a strong focus helped Tata Finance to overtake well established brands and become the number one in FDs in the late 1990s.

Tata Finance is now poised to make strong, but careful moves into newer territories like auto loans, as the middle class customer expands his basket of needs.

Tata Finance: Brand Building Tips

Selling a parity service product like fixed deposits calls for a strong 'corporate brand' support coupled with an emotional pay-off that goes beyond the product offering. Tata Finance fixed deposits managed to leverage the 'corporate brand' and position the offering on an emotional platform of 'peace of mind'.

FENNER—Performance Power from Fenner

In 1861, an Englishman named Fenner started a company to manufacture leather belting for use in manufacturing industries, for the purpose of power transmission. The product design was simple, consisting of a belt which connected a large pulley wheel to a smaller one, facilitating transmission of power. In the late 1920s, JH Fenner & Co. started operations in India, bringing the by-now world famous Fenner V-Belts to India. The success of its V-Belts established JH Fenner & Co. as a leader in mechanical power transmission with offerings for diverse industries.

In 1987, the firm renamed as Fenner (India) Ltd., was taken over by the JK Organisation. Subsequently, the pace of modernisation and diversification accelerated. By the early 1990s, Fenner had become the leader in mechanical power transmission with different product offerings for diverse industries, with a turnover of Rs 250 crores. Fenner products ranged from V-Belts and power transmission products to conveyer belting, auto belts and oil seals to electronic controls and material handling systems for textiles.

BACKGROUND

Over the years, Fenner had developed and enjoyed a strong brand equity. Its expertise and strength in technology, quality and service were widely recognised. Despite this, however, Fenner, suffered from an image problem.

In spite of the fact that all of Fenner's products were leaders in their category. Fenner was seen only as a V-Belt company. For instance, its auto products division comprising auto belts, and oil seals commanded a market share of more than 70 per cent. Likewise, its conveyer belting systems, engineering products, industrial electronics, material handling systems and other offerings were all industry leaders in their respective categories. The perception of Fenner as a V-Belt company started its operations with the manufacture of V-Belts. On the way, Fenner's achievements in other areas of power transmission went largely unnoticed. This was largely due to low media visibility accorded to other product divisions such as material handling systems, conveyor belting systems etc., which by virtue of their

PUBLIC RELATIONS

Unpaid media coverage. Relationship–communication efforts aimed at various publics, customers, trade, government, employees... all this encompasses Public Relations.

A much misunderstood term, often confused with press relations or press releases, Public Relations is emerging as a true profession in India. The influx of global majors has given the industry its much needed impetus.

What is the objective of a PR programme? When it wanted to make an impact in India, Intel wanted PR to bring it into the media spotlight, at regular intervals, in a systematic manner, over a long period of time. The objective defined the scope, depth and duration of the programme.

A well orchestrated programme can give the brand and the company coverage worth millions.

Often PR, coupled with mass media, pays off extremely well. The consumer gets doubly influenced if he reads about the brand in the editorial columns as well as the ad!

Before setting out to brief the PR agency it is necessary to be clear on:

- What are the objectives of the programme?
- Who are the target publics?
- What will be the duration of the programme?
- What will be the measurement of results?

Source: FCB-Ulka

industrial nature, relied largely on direct selling. Even the auto products division, which produced auto belts and oil seals for mass use, targeted its products at the original equipment segment and not the replacement market.

Fenner was clear that it had to create a strong image of the company as a technologically advanced leader in power transmission, to exploit the opportunities for achieving its growth plans. FCB-Ulka, which at that point of time, was handling the account was entrusted with the task of building the Fenner corporate brand across the spectrum of power transmission products.

The Communication Task

An informal study conducted by the agency revealed that Fenner's products enjoyed a positive image among different users of the various target industries. However, except for the common denominator of V-Belts, users in a specific industry were largely unaware of Fenner's other offerings targeted at other user industries. This called for advertising that would change consumer perceptions about Fenner and create a strong image for the brand, among the target audience.

The communication objective was defined as creating and strengthening Fenner's image as a technologically sound multi-product, multi-division company which is a leader in power transmission.

The Target Audience

Findings also revealed that since Fenner's products were industrial products of high value with high involvement levels, there were several members with varying profiles influencing the purchase decision-making process. The profile of these members ranged from shop floor engineers to purchase managers to managing directors. The communication, therefore, would have to address people at different levels in different industries. In addition, it also had to address other target audiences, such as prospective customers, technical consultants, financial institutions/investors and business associates.

The Advertising—Strategy Execution

Given Fenner's strong image, it was decided to leverage the company's strengths in the areas of product quality, reliability and technology. In line with the communication objective, the proposition was defined as "Fenner-the leader in mechanical power trans-mission with a range of products offering unbeatable performance". To amplify the proposition,

> ### They Said So
>
> *"Advertising is much like war, minus the venom. Or much, if you prefer, like a game of chess. We are usually out to capture others' citadels or garner others' trade."*
>
> •**Claude Hopkins,**
> *"Scientific Advertising"*

a multi-ad campaign was developed to focus on the performance of Fenner's range of products which catered to the needs of diverse industries.

The multi-ad campaign comprised five black and white ads, each making a strong leadership statement while establishing Fenner as a multi-product, multi-division company. Each ad had a visual of the product and the headline talking about product quality and reliability and the brief body copy highlighting the various divisions of Fenner. Each ad had a common continuing thought '... Performance Power from Fenner' and signed off with the baseline 'Fenner, the front-runner'.

Media Objectives and Strategy

Keeping in mind the communication task and the target audience to be reached, business dailies and magazines were used as the primary media. In addition, a few specialist and general interest English magazines were also chosen. The media strategy employed a concentrated burst in the first phase of the launch followed by continuous advertising in magazines to ensure visibility.

The advertising campaign ran for seven months in 1994-95 and was repeated in 1995-96.

Evaluation of the Campaign

A post-campaign survey was conducted to gauge the effectiveness of the campaign. A detailed structured questionnaire was administered to a sample of respondents belonging to the target audience. The main findings of the study were:

- Over 70 per cent of the respondents perceived Fenner as a multi-division company with expertise in mechanical power transmission.
- 60 per cent of the respondents recalled the campaign with little or no aid.
- V-Belt, auto belts and conveyor belt ads enjoyed the highest recall.
- 65 per cent of the respondents identified with one or more Fenner products from the campaign.

Heard-in-the-Agency

"Oh that meeting. Nobody told you ...

The client was so impressed with the advertising,

he wants to now make sure his product delivers.

So for the next 8 months,

he wants to only concentrate on the product.

But ..... hey, great work!"

Press Ad
Fenner
"After 3,65,000 arrivals and departures..."

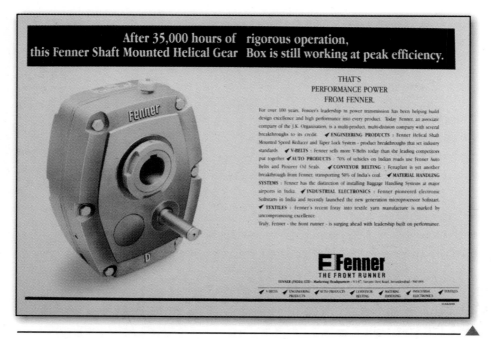

Press Ad
Fenner
"After 35,000 hours of rigorous operation..."

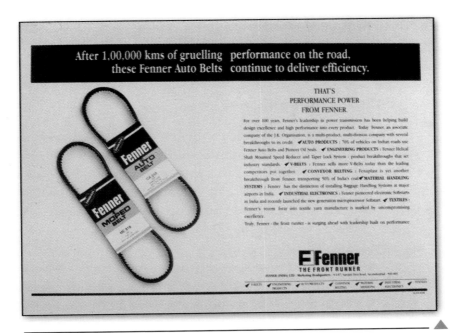

Press Ad
Fenner
"After 1,00,000 kms of gruelling..."

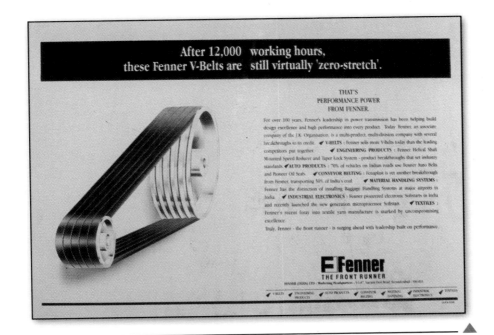

Press Ad
Fenner
"After 12,000 working hours..."

- Among industrial product companies which were rated for their advertising, Fenner stood ninth. The list had names like L&T, Kirloskar, Siemens, BHEL, Dunlop, GEC, BEML etc.

Follow-Through

Fenner's corporate brand campaign has had its impact in the short run. In order to maximise the brand building efforts it will be necessary to follow this through in the long term with regular brand building inputs. Fenner is planning to keep a part of its marketing budgets for focused 'brand' advertising–to continue to build up the brand salience.

Fenner: Brand Building Tips

Engineering products, marketed under a strong umbrella brand often need the support of an 'umbrella' brand promise. It is then critical to link the various offerings, like Fenner did with the slogan, 'That's performance power from Fenner', to leverage the message.

CASE STUDY

TATA LUCENT—New Frontiers in Telecommunication

Telecommunication in India has historically been highly regulated. The opening up of the telecom sector has taken place in phases. The first milestone was in 1984-85, when telecom equipment manufacturing was opened up to private Indian operators. This heralded the entry of a host of players including Tata Telecom into the manufacturing of EPABXs. However, over time, most of these manufacturers, except Crompton Greaves, Tata Telecom, and the C-DoT licensees shut down their operations. The C-DoT licensees refocused their business towards the manufacture of RAXs (Rural Exchanges) for which they found a ready market in DoT, which was looking for suppliers of these exchanges at this time.

The second milestone came in 1993-94, when the market for telecom services was opened up to private operators. This included basic, paging and cellular services and signalled the Indian government's seriousness in de-regulating the telecom sector. This resulted in the beginning of a new phase in equipment manufacturing as well, which saw the entry of multinational telecom majors such as Ericsson, Siemens, Alcatel and Nortel in a big way into India, with a wide range of telecom equipment.

Tata Telecom, in the meantime, began to suffer from the associations of being a homegrown entity. Recognising the need to have access to cutting edge technology, the company entered into a collaboration with AT&T for a range of telecom products. In 1996, AT&T went through a major corporate restructuring, which resulted in its splitting into three companies, of which Lucent Technologies was one. Lucent Technologies combined the systems and technology units that were formerly a part of AT&T with the research and development capabilities of Bell Labs. In 1997, a joint venture called Tata-Lucent Technologies Limited was born to offer a wide range of telecom products including network systems, microelectronics, communication software, business communication systems and consumer products in India.

The Telecom Spectrum

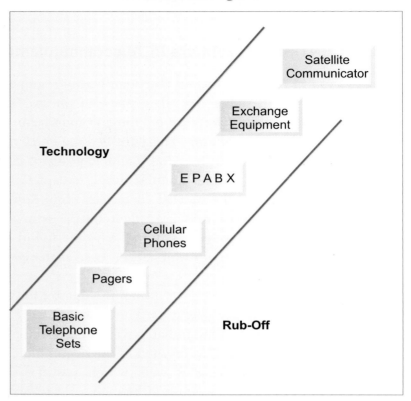

THE PROBLEM

Feedback from consumers showed that each of the joint venture (JV) partners suffered from certain limitations. While Tata was a well recognised name, within the realm of telecom it was associated only with EPABXs. Siemens, Nortel, Alcatel and Ericsson were seen as a cut above, as they associated with a whole host of other high profile telecom categories like cellular handsets and networking. These were categories which had seen major advances in recent years and were, therefore, seen as exciting and happening categories. EPABXs on the other hand, had not seen any revolutionary technological breakthroughs in recent years and hence were seen as fairly run-of-the-mill products with nothing particularly hi-tech about them. Tata Telecom suffered from its solitary association with this category and was consequently seen as low-tech. The MNC competitors enjoyed the rub-off of their association with more visible and 'hi-tech' categories. They had also

Brand building is possible through creation of a property that reinforces brand image. One such example is the Guinness Book of Records, which is today almost an independent brand. So is our own Filmfare Awards.

In a country that worships cricket there existed no official awards (whereas in the film arena there were numerous awards, Filmfares, National Awards, Screen etc.) Ceat, India's premier tyre brand latched on to the opportunity offered by cricket.

Ceat Cricket Ratings was born. With the help of a professional cricket agency, rating methodologies were developed. Tie-ups with sports channels started giving Ceat Cricket Rating the exposure it needed to become the legitimate Cricket Rating System. This was then followed by the selection of the Ceat Cricketer of the Year—who was crowned at a glittering function in Bombay. The event has now become a brand and this brand is further strengthening the brand salience of Ceat tyres!

Source: FCB-Ulka

managed to build up awareness and positive associations in a short period of time, thereby repositioning Tata Telecom as old and not 'with-it'.

While AT&T was not only well-known but seen as the first name in telecommunications and a pioneer across the world, Lucent, the other entity in the joint venture, was a completely new name.

THE OPPORTUNITY

Popularly known as the one-year old company with a 120-year old heritage, Lucent Technologies brought with it the Bell Labs ancestry. A revered institution the world over, Bell Labs has changed the course of history in the field of business communications through its numerous pathbreaking inventions, starting with, of course, the telephone. While Lucent was unknown, Bell Labs was fairly well-known and associated with the forefront of technology.

The Tata name, too, had several positive attributes mainly because it had been around in the Indian telecom market for the longest time. Being a leader with the largest installed base of EPABXs in India, it was seen as trustworthy with a fairly good after-sales service, and as a brand with lasting power. Thus, it provided the reinforcement that customers seek for large investments such as telecom equipment.

The Communication Strategy

In a category requiring large investments and substantial follow-up, the corporate image played an important role in the decision-making process. Thus, while there was product-centred advertising for specific products, there was a need to create something bigger at the corporate level. Research had shown that image and association with technology was also linked to visibility in media. A high profile launch of the JV was decided on to pitch the corporate in the same league as the MNC majors. The route for doing this was through playing up the Bell Labs connection to give the company a hi-tech sheen. The communication task was not sales oriented, but focused on corporate image. The target audience was a small set of Chief Information Officers (CIOs) and MDs involved in making decisions on large telecom investments.

Selling a High-end Telecom Product

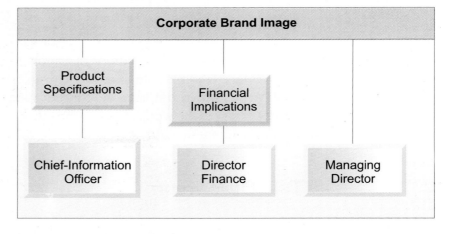

Creative Strategy and Execution

The challenge was to create a multi-layered communication establishing a series of connections between various entities and their achievements. The achievements and pioneering spirit of Bell Labs had to be highlighted, which

BRAND BUILDING ADVERTISING ■

had then to be associated with Lucent. Further, the communication had to announce the launch of the JV and reinforce the Tata values of reliability and trust.

All this came together in the key creative thought around which the campaign revolved: pioneering new frontiers in communication.

To establish Lucent's credentials, the innovations for which Bell Labs is famous were put up front. Four ads described four landmark patents of Bell Labs; viz., the telephone, the transistor, digital cellular transmitters and network theory. To further establish the relevance of these for today and the future, their impact on modern and future telecommunications was then expounded upon. In execution terms, this was done through a two-tiered headline. The visuals reinforced the telecom landmarks for which Bell Labs was responsible, but care was also taken to give them a certain fluidity for making the campaign friendly rather than intimidating. The device of a visiting card visual, clearly connecting Bell Labs Innovations with Tata Lucent and Tata Lucent with its parents, was the signature of this campaign, which served to sum up the connections between the various entities.

Since the target for the communication was highly focused, the print medium was chosen. The vehicles used were business publications and trade journals—considered serious reading by the target consumers. The choice of media thus gave the communication a certain credibility and weight. Large sizes and colour were used to import a sense of vastness and a larger than life image.

Heard-in-the-Agency

"*Great Script. Oh my God, really Great Script.*

But where's the idea?"

They Said So

"It has been stressed that advertising most often has an informative role as compared with the legitimising role of word-of-mouth influence. Thus one primary task of advertising is to communicate relevant product information and, hopefully, to persuade the consumer to purchase the product or service offered. At other times, however, advertising plays a much more decisive role and actually triggers the decision. The marketing implications of these functions are sharply different."

• **James F. Engel, Roger D. Blackwell, David T. Kaollat**
"Consumer Behaviour"

RESULT

Tata Lucent is a well recognised and respected entity. Lucent Technologies is well known as the progeny of Bell Labs and is identified as being at the

Press Ad
Tata Telecom
"In 1929 Bell Labs..."

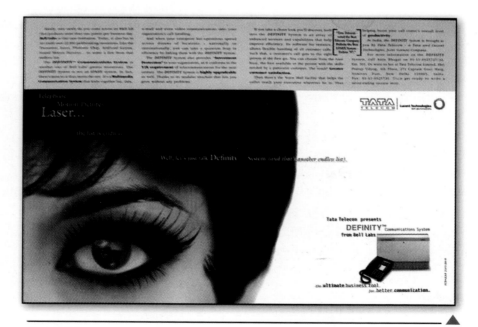

Press Ad
Tata Telecom
"Telephone. Motion Pictures. Laser..."

BRAND BUILDING ADVERTISING ■

Press Ad
Tata Telecom
"Way back in '86 Bell Labs..."

Press Ad
Tata Telecom
"Since 1925 Bell Labs..."

frontiers of telecommunications technology. The joint venture has also had a positive rub-off on Tata Telecom which is now seen as being technologically savvy in addition to being the leader in EPABXs.

Tata Lucent now has an established practice of apportioning a significant part of its marketing budgets to corporate umbrella brand advertising, which goes on to support the specific product advertising.

Tata Lucent: Brand Building Tips

High value, high technology products are primarily sold on the corporate brand 'aura'. Therefore, even before product advertising, it is important to build the corporate brand's credibility, like that of Tata Lucent, or at least do a combination of the two with a greater focus on the corporate brand's achievements.

Brand Building
Rural Inputs Advertising

"Come with us to the fields, or go with our brothers to the sea and cast your net. For the land and the sea shall be bountiful to you even as to us."

• Kahlil Gibran

India is still an agricultural economy. Over 30 per cent of its GDP comes from the agricultural sector, as compared to developed countries where the figure is less than 10 per cent. Agriculture is also the one sector of the economy which is at times over-protected, and at times over-exploited. Rural inputs marketing offers its own set of challenges and opportunities to astute marketing professionals.

RURAL INPUTS

Often rural marketing is confused with rural inputs marketing. So it is probably apt at this stage to define the two.

Rural marketing refers to marketing activities aimed at households living in rural areas, as defined by the census of India. For all practical purposes, they are no different from their urban brethren expect for the fact that they live in villages. Rural marketing can be undertaken for soaps, toothpastes, detergents, fans, scooters, TVs etc.

Rural inputs marketing refers to products and services that a farmer uses to produce his crop. The term rural inputs marketing is thus in a way, a subset of rural marketing. The similarity, however ends there. Rural inputs range from an expensive tractor to urea which is almost a commodity.

The farmer buys these products in very different ways.

But first let us try and look at the various types of rural inputs:

- Heavy Equipment
    - Tractors, Tillers
    - Pump sets, Irrigation systems
- Agricultural Inputs
    - Fertilisers
    - Hybrid seeds
    - Pesticides
- Services
    - Farm input loans

How Does Advertising Work?

The age of the 'illiterate', 'marginal', 'subsistence-level' farmer will be over very soon. We will have among us, intelligent, smart, larger-land-holding farmers who see farming as a business venture, often working out cost-benefit ratios before deciding on the crop, the hybrid, the inputs etc.

Advertising in its conventional, mass-media dominated style will have to be re-defined to suit the farmer community. It is necessary to see the farmer not just as an emotional animal, as shown in old movies, but as possessing a combination of emotional and rational facilities. But how to communicate with the farmer will continue to be complex.

How does a farmering decide? What are the rules influencing decision-making? What influences him at what stage? How does he see conventional advertising?

The purchase of farming inputs is a high-involvement activity for the farmer. This is true of farm equipment which might cost thousands of rupees as also of hybrid seeds that cost just a few hundred rupees. The same is true of the purchase of pesticides and fertilisers as well. What role does advertising play?

Farmers are always looking forward to obtaining information about products that help them improve their crop yield. But this information has to come from a credible source—not just from anywhere. The most effective medium of communication is word-of-mouth. If the farmer hears the right message from the right source, he will be willing to try out new methods.

India's Green Revolution was triggered by the use of messages targeted at opinion leaders at the village level. This then led to the trickle down effect of information flowing towards the target hierarchy. (Unfortunately the opposite happened with family planning efforts.)

Brand Building Rural Inputs Advertising

Building a rural inputs brand is, as expected, more difficult than, say, building a consumer product brand. But once established, the brand has a longer life span. Given the absence of specialised media aimed at farmers, and the prohibitive cost of TV advertising, the job becomes even more difficult.

As in the case of other branding exercises, in the case of rural inputs as well, the key is to decide on the branding architecture - what is the umbrella brand? Will this brand be the mother brand ? Or will it just be an endorser brand?

For the last 50 years, farm inputs have relied heavily on visual symbols to talk to farmers:

- Elephant   –   FACT Fertilizers
- Moon   –   ICI Fertilizers
- Man and Horse   –   Zuari

This has changed with the advent of sophisticated hybrid seeds and pesticides. These are, by and large, sold as brands—farmers, however, use symbols to identify brands—Ciba Geigy was identified as the 'Sun' brand!

The next task is to define the core, values/images of the brand —will the brand be presented as a scientist? A friend? A toughie?

Then comes the task of offering the brand promise. Better crop yield! Less pest trouble! Prosperity!

The communication has to have a strong dose of 'how-to-do-it', since it is a high involvement purchase and farmers are looking for information, not just for a feel-good effect.

Given the fact that word-of-mouth is the most credible source of information for the farmer, advertising can attempt to be as close to word-of-mouth as possible without becoming boring.

In addition to conventional media like press and TV, farm input brands will have to look at new areas of advertising. Outdoor publicity and point-of-purchase (POP) material are important. Specialised media like video vans, touring-talkies (small cinema halls) and numerous other opportunities will have to be explored. Direct mail is yet another medium that offers a lot of potential for reaching the targeted farmers.

All in all, building a rural input brand is a challenging, difficult task. But with an increase in sophistication, literacy levels, and availability of media, and with segmentation becoming commonplace, the day is not too far when India starts getting its share of special farm input magazines and a farm input TV channel!

CASES

The following section has one case on farm inputs, viz. hybrid seeds. The case attempts to present, in a nutshell, the complexities of marketing a farm input. The case is to be seen only as a small subset of activities that went on to build this brand.

CASE STUDY

NOVARTIS– Protecting the Farmer's "Cotton Cash"

Cotton. The ultimate cash crop. The target for every pesticide brand. But how can these brands break through the clutter and reach their target farmers? How can they make the target farmer listen to their offers and react positively?

THE COMPANY

Novartis India Limited is an affiliate of Novartis AG, headquartered in Basel, Switzerland. Novartis was formed with the worldwide merger of two Swiss giants–Ciba Geigy and Sandoz (FCB-Ulka's association with Ciba Giegy dates back to the 1970s).

Novartis is positioned as the "world's leading life sciences company". The company has business operations in the areas of pharmaceuticals, crop protection, seeds, animal health and vision care.

The company's Crop Protection Division, which is in the business of manufacturing and marketing of crop pesticides, is one of the key business units contributing about Rs 230 crore of the total company turnover of Rs 600 crore (1997). Novartis is the second largest player in the pesticides market, with a vision of becoming the number one in the market by the year 2001.

THE PESTICIDES MARKET

The total pesticide market was estimated at Rs 2800 crore in 1997 and the market was growing at a rate of 10 per cent p.a.

The key players in the market are:

- Rallis — 11.8% M.S.
- Novartis — 8.6% M.S.
- United Phosphorus — 8.4% M.S.
- Gharda — 8.3% M.S.
- Bayer — 7.5% M.S.
- Agrero — 6.9% M.S.

Unlike that of consumer products, the pesticides market is diverse and complex. In a nutshell, pesticides are used by farmers to get rid of pests. But the type of pesticide used would depend on the following factors:

1. Type of pest
   - worms
   - fungus
   - weeds

2. Type of crops
   - foodgrains
     - wheat
     - paddy etc.
   - cash crops
     - cotton
     - tobacco etc.

INFOLINE

CELEBRATION BRANDING

Brands can create events. And events can be used to create brands. These could be called 'Celebration Brands'. A World Cup watch. An Independence Day Pen.

India celebrated 50 years of independence on 15 August 1997. A number of companies had special campaigns and special events to celebrate 50 years of independence.

One company decided to use the occasion to create a brand. Parrys, India's largest confectionery company thought of launching a brand of toffee to celebrate 50 years of Indian independence. Delving into the company's records revealed that Parry's used to make high-energy toffees for the armed forces as EFR (Emergency Flying Ration).

On June 15, 1997 a decision was taken to launch this toffee as Parry's Indian.

Packaging and positioning was finalized in just seven days. A new commercial was shot. The brand rolled out into the market on August 1, 1997. Numerous schools across the country celebrated India's 50th Independence Day with Parry's Indian!

Source: FCB-Ulka

- vegetables and fruits
  - mangoes
  - grapes etc.
- plantation crops
  - tea
  - coffee etc.
3. Geographical differences
  - South
  - North
4. Seasonal differences
  - *rabi*
  - *kharif*

Pesticides Categories

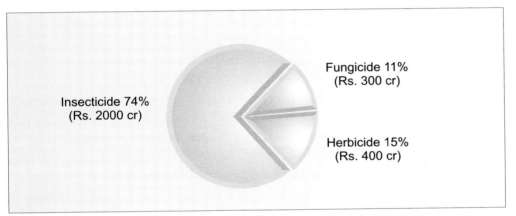

Insecticides account for almost 75 per cent of the pesticide market. Indian farmers still use manual methods to deal with weeds– internationally the herbicide market is also very large.

Two crops, cotton and paddy, account for over 50 per cent of the insecticide market. The balance is accounted for by all the other crops put together!

Andhra Pradesh (AP), Karnataka and Tamil Nadu account for a major share, of over 50 per cent of the insecticide market. The other key markets are Punjab, Haryana, Gujarat and Maharashtra.

The Target Consumers

Given the market scenario, the prime target consumers of insecticides are farmers growing cotton, rice and wheat in the key states.

As in consumer products, they are not the 'same' everywhere. Their behaviours differ with their affluence levels which are reflected in their land-holding patterns.

The larger (land-holding) farmers are more educated and see farming almost as an industrial-business activity. They are knowledgeable and well-versed with modern farming methods and techno-logies. They would not normally fit into the typical stereotype of the simplistic 'sentimental' farmer portrayed in Indian films!

The large majority of medium and small (land-holding) farmers fit into the stereotype a little more. They are semi-literate and depend on word-of-mouth to learn about new developments.

In the pesticides market, certain myths exist like "spraying more will reduce pests". Because of these myths the farmer tends to go in for the cheapest product and over-uses it on his crops (This also happens in the case of fertilisers where the prices for certain types of fertilisers are subsidised).

There is also a strong "herd mentality" among farmers. Farmers often adopt practices on the basis of word-of-mouth, at times blindly.

"Seeing is believing" is the farmers' *mantra*. Nothing works better than a 'demonstration plot' and getting the farmers to see it for themselves. At times two plots, side by side, can get a whole district to switch to a new product.

The farmer also has an established network of people to rely on for information. It may consists of the *panchayat* president, the dealer, the 'big farmers' or the farm advisor (from an agro-input company).

Given the market scenario, the pesticide marketeer has to plan his complex marketing communication strategy to reach the target farmer, at the right time, with the right promise!

Novartis: Targetting Cotton

Cotton is the most important cash crop grown in western, central and southern parts of India. Cotton is also highly susceptible to pest attacks, and of these pests, Heliothis (Ballworm) is the commonest and most menacing.

Novartis, after extensive research, developed two insecticides, Curacron and Polytrin C44. These worked in tandem to control the Ballworm population at various stages. The same insecticides were also effective against a whole range of other pests that attacked other crops.

Farmers are targeted by pesticide marketeers for all kinds of pesticides aimed at all kinds of pests. Most of the brands offer an 'umbrella' protection against 'all pests' for 'all crops'. This has led farmers to treat pesticides as commodities and to create their own admixtures for each crop and each season.

How can one break this habit? Will the farmer be ready to listen to a 'specialist' offering? Will he be ready to accept a 'brand', and in this case 'two brands' as a combined 'specialist' product?

The Novartis marketing team felt that it was worthwhile to narrow the focus of advertising and go after the 'one crop—one pest' formula with a 'dual brand' strategy. The benefits of this strategy far outweighed the risks.

Curacron and Polytrin C 44: The Cotton Specialists

Novartis positioned Curacron and Polytrin C44 as 'the cotton specialists'. They worked in combination: Curacron worked in the early stages to kill off the eggs and larvae, and during the flowering period, Polytrin C44 gave the crop added protection.

This 'brand combination' was aimed at exploiting some of the farmers deep-rooted beliefs such as 'no single pesticide is enough', 'the more the better'. At the same time, the brands were formulated to work on various 'forms' in which the pest attacked the crops.

The key target consumers were the progressive farmer, pesticides dealer and opinion leaders.

Then came the challenge of developing a communication platform. The agency and the Novartis team discussed various options. Research had revealed several interesting points:

- Almost all brands used a very rational approach offering 'generic' benefits and higher yield as a payoff.
- Farmers were showing some concern about the harmful effects of pesticides.
- The 'increased yield' claim is often untenable when used for pesticides (hybrid seeds and fertilisers have a major claim to that promise).
- The complete elimination of Ballworms was perceived as 'impossible' by farmers.

So the advertising had to work at an 'emotional' level to appeal to the farmers.

Since cotton was the ultimate cash crop, the offer made to the farmer was, "Save your cash from the attack of the Ballworm".

The communication literally showed a currency note being eaten away by an 'over-eager' ballworm!

The objective of the campaign was to create awareness for Curacron and Polytrin C44, and position them as 'the cotton specialists'.

Unlike consumer products advertising, mass media (like press or TV) alone are not enough for farm inputs advertising.

Novartis used a whole gamut of communication vehicles to deliver the 'cotton specialist' message. These included:

- POP material put up at dealer points
- Outdoor publicity like wall paintings
- Farmer meets where the concept was explained with the help of visual aids, films etc.
- Booklets—an innovative flicker booklet was distributed to farmers—creating interest, albeit in a different manner.

The communication package was created in Hindi, Punjabi, Tamil, Kannada, Telugu, Marathi and Gujarati.

The Novartis marketing team got the entire campaign orchestrated to target the key states for the *kharif* season of 1997. 'Protect your cash with Curacron and Polytrin C44' was the unifying message transmitted all around.

With most other brands offering multiple benefits—multiple crops — multiple pests, the Novartis promise stood out. It struck a chord with the farmers because of its rational appeal (two pesticides—not just one) and the emotional payoff ('protect your cash').

RESULT

Curacron is the number one pesticide in cotton and Polytrin C44 and Curacron together comprise a formidable brand pair, touching sales of Rs 25 crore, within two years of the product launch.

In fact, today the demand is outstripping production, with Novartis receiving advance 'pay orders' for the brands—possibly a 'first' in the ultra-crowded pesticides market!

Novartis–Farmer

The film is an animation and opens with a woman carrying a stack of paddy on her head.

Close-up of the farmer's hand protecting the crop.

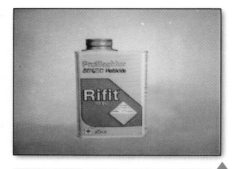

Cut to an old pack the product Rifit from Ciba-Geigy.
VO: Your trusted Rifit in a new improved formulation and attractive packaging.

VO: Healthy crops and a higher yield is every farmer's dream.

Farmer's hand and the crop dissolves to form the Novartis logo.
VO: The world's number one life science company.

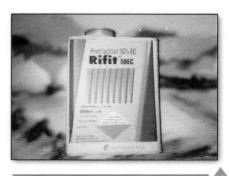

The pack starts rotating and dissolves to become a new pack.
VO: Our developments are inspired by your needs.

VO: And Novartis promises to do everything to help you achieve your dream.

VO: Novartis is committed to R&D in finding new solutions to your problems.

The film ends with the Novartis logo over a swaying paddy field.

Novartis Press Ad.
"Before Ballworms eat up your crops..."

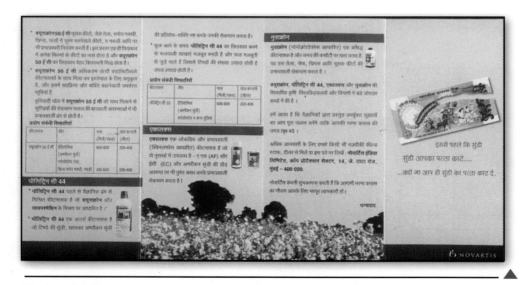

Novartis Leaflet

BRAND BUILDING ADVERTISING ■

Novartis Press Ad.
"Now prosperity comes to your doorstep..."

Novartis Press Ad.
"Wish for a healthy crop of paddy..."

Advertising Beyond Brands

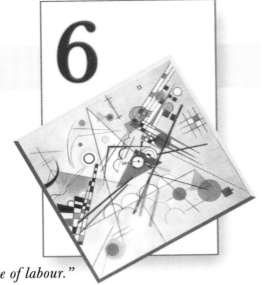

"God sells us all things at the price of labour."
• Leonardo Da Vinci

A dvertising is often called upon to go beyond brands and address larger issues. These could be socially relevant issues that no single brand can take on single handedly.

One of the oldest and long running campaigns in the United States of America is the campaign to prevent forest fires. These fires, largely caused by campers and 'picnickers', have been significantly brought down by the "Smokey–The Bear" campaign done by FCB.

At the next level is the campaign conducted by industrial bodies that go beyond brands to benefit the entire industry. These range from organised efforts to increase the use of steel, to selling more milk.

THE LARGER ROLE OF ADVERTISING

Advertising plays two broad roles in the socio-economic landscape of a country.

At an economic level, advertising stimulates demand, educates consumers about new products, increases competition and improves standards of living by helping to bring new products to the consumer.

At a social level, advertising plays upon, derives from and contributes to the social texture of a country. Advertising mirrors society and society mirrors advertising. Several social changes are brought about or aided by advertising. Advertising creates role models who can, in turn, create societal change. These models could be the working mother or the husband who cooks!

Role of Advertising

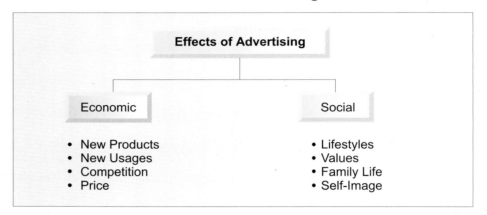

Above all these factors are issues about the 'ethics' of advertising. Does it stir unwanted desires? Does it sell unnecessary products? Does it target messages at minds which are not yet ready for them?

In a developing country like India, these questions are asked even more loudly, at times leading to regulatory action—like the ban on infant cereal advertising over television, or the rule that stipulates that advertising of female hygiene products (sanitary napkins) can be advertised only after 9 pm.

While these issues persist, advertising is also used to sell the concept of family planning and other social service messages. How should one use a condom? How can one protect oneself from AIDS? How can one prevent and eradicate polio with the Pulse Polio campaign?

Advertising is, doubtless, a fuel that boosts the economy, by helping to bring new products faster and more efficiently to consumers, by helping to achieve the economies of scale faster and by helping to break product monopolies.

Advertising also helps promote several social causes, if used prudently. Regulatory authorities and, more importantly, self-regulatory authorities have started playing a more imporant role in helping advertising stay within the boundaries of what is ethically, morally correct.

BRAND BUILDING ADVERTISING ■

Role of Advertising Beyond Brands

Advertising is a competitive weapon, that helps one brand to stand up, against competition from other brands.

Advertising is often used to sell generic products. Sometimes these are "larger brands" while at times they are nameless products. The Indian Government, over the last 20 years, has been able to build the brand of "Darjeeling tea" in the international markets, just as "Colombian coffee" is a recognised "large brand".

In the domestic scenario too, manufacturers of specific products have come together to promote a larger cause. We have seen this happen diverse products like steel, jute, egg and milk.

However, these efforts are often short-lived and soon suffer from the "who will pay" syndrome. The more successful social service compaigns have had regular supports in terms of funding and the involvement of an active nodal body that drives the campaign.

CASES

One of the most successful and visible 'beyond brand' advertising campaigns in recent times has been the milk promotion campaign by NDDB. This case provides a glimpse of how it was developed and the effect it has had on the perception and consumption of milk in the country.

Doodh Doodh—Wonderful: Glassful Real Taste of Milk

The Indian dairy scene has witnessed a magical transformation- from the time when we did not have enough milk for our own consumption to todays scenario when we are exporting milk products. The credit for this turnaround, in no small measure, goes to the National Dairy Development Board (NDDB). Since its inception in 1965, NDDB has helped in the formation of more than 72,000 village level milk cooperatives spread throughout the country, with a membership of 10 million producers. Recently, India made history when it became the largest milk producer in the world.

In spite of a long tradition of drinking milk, of late, this trend has been on the decline, especially amongst the urban youth who form a significant market for the product. Milk is being perceived by them as a 'plain', 'boring', drink or mistakenly among the health-conscious, as 'fattening'. This attitudinal block resulted in more milk being earmarked for the production of milk products or as an intermediary in tea or coffee, than for consumption as a drink. The economic ramifications of this trend are, needless to say, alarming for the farmers who needed incentives to produce higher quantities of milk.

FCB-Ulka was entrusted with the task of changing urban attitudes towards milk and replace the 'boring' perception with the 'cool' one. In a pathbreaking campaign that had youngsters doing high fives and saying 'yo' to milk, and mothers making their kids drink to the 'taste of life', the agency created a legend that has set new standards in effective advertising while elevating the creative benchmark, several notches.

BACKGROUND

The National Dairy Development Board (NDDB) was set up in 1965 under the Chairmanship of Dr. Verghese Kurien, to replicate the success of the Kaira District Cooperative Milk Producers Union (AMUL) of Gujarat, all over the country and make it self-sufficient in milk. The Board has exceeded that expectation many times over considering the fact that the 7,27,000 village milk cooperatives that NDDB helped to create have merged into 170 district level unions and 23 state federations, and supply over 25 per cent of the total milk produced in the country.

With a total international share of 11 per cent India leads the world in milk production, a feat accomplished in great measure due to NDDB's efforts. Today, even as the rest of the world presents a dismal picture in milk production with a decline in output, the Indian dairy industry is growing at an impressive rate of 5 per cent every year. With such positive trends at play, the country is also set to emerge as an exporter of dairy products.

NDDB: A BRIEF HISTORY

The inception of NDDB traces its roots to the formation of the Kaira District Cooperative Milk Producers Union way back in 1946.

INFOLINE

DRESSING IT UP

The 1990s have seen Indian men dressing it up, in fancy new labels! Increased options, high power marketing and a white-collar dress regimen have made Indian men take a fresh look at their wardrobe.

A study done among 1500 males in Bombay, Delhi and Bangalore in 1998, reveals some interesting insights.

Indian men have started buying ready-made garments in large numbers. Almost 70 per cent of the men in the 16 to 49 age group, belonging to SEC A and B buy branded products.

But do they only use 'branded' products?

No The penetration of branded shirts is much higher than that of branded trousers. Could this be because Indian men, given their height-size mix, find trousers to be ill-fitting? Or could this be because shirts have been available in a 'branded' form for years with pioneers like Zodiac showing the way?

Branded casual wear too has caught on, with the highest penetration of 85 per cent, reported in Delhi.

But in the midst of all the action from global brands, a number of Indian brands offering a combination of value and style are holding their own!

Source: *Brand Equity, Economic Times*
November 11–17, 98

As with any commodity, the producer got a raw deal in the sale of milk, whereas the trader and the middleman made good money. Under the govern-ment of Bombay's milk scheme, M/s Polson and the middlemen filled their coffers, whereas the poor farmers remained in abject poverty. Their helplessness was compounded by the fact that milk, being a perishable commodity, has to be readily disposed of. Although aware of their exploitation, the farmers of Kheda district accepted it as their fate, till Sardar Vallabhbhai Patel sent Morarji Desai to help them organise milk cooperatives. When the government refused to buy milk from the infant cooperative, the farmers unitedly refused to sell milk to the trader as well, and for 15 days not a drop of milk reached Bombay. The government was forced to capitulate and accept the farmers' demand that milk been bought from them as well. Thus was set in motion the Kaira District Cooperative Milk Producers' Union which is today better known as Amul.

A modest beginning with 250 litres of milk from two villages grew to an impressive collection of 5000 litres per day by 1948. The increase in production, more so during the 'flush' winter season when production is two-and-a-half times that in summer, exceeded the demand and new avenues were explored so that the farmer was not forced to sell the surplus to middlemen at low rates. Diversification into value-added products like butter and milk powder, and products such as baby food and condensed milk was undertaken successfully.

The success of this cooperative was noticed, and recognised by the Government of India when it set up the NDDB for replicating the success of this cooperative venture. The objective before NDDB was to make the country self-sufficient in milk production through the formation of the 'Anand pattern' cooperative structures.

Towards this end, Operation Flood was launched to increase milk handling and production, especially in milk deficient areas. By 1996, it had covered 72,744 cooperative societies, with an Operation Flood membership of over 9,30,000 members. Milk production reached an all-time high of 72 billion litres at the end of Operation Flood in 1996.

BRAND BUILDING ADVERTISING ■

The White Revolution—Some Results

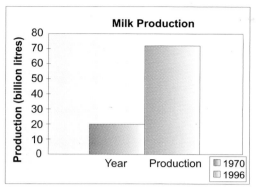

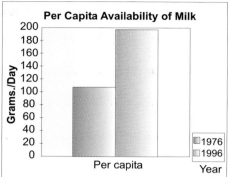

Snapshots from the Milk Market

- The unorganised sector accounts for 70 per cent of the total milk produced.
- Private dairies, which are a part of the organised sector, have mushroomed after 1991, in the post-liberalisation era.
- The dairy business is characterised by a cyclical nature. The production in winter is two-and-a-half times that of summer.

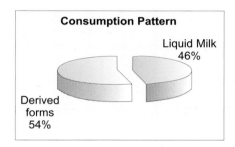

Thus, every summer is characterised by a supply crunch as the demand is constant.

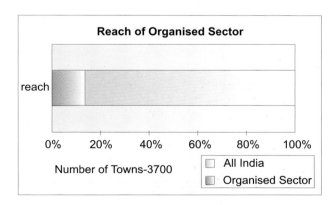

■ Only 46 per cent of the total production is directly consumed as liquid milk.

   ■ The organised sector supplies milk to only 600 towns in India.

The range of milk available in the organised market:

1. Packaging:
   ■ Plastic pouches
   ■ Glass bottles
   ■ Tetrapacks
2. Fat content:
   ■ Toned
   ■ Double Toned
   ■ Standardized
   ■ Full Cream
3. Packed milk has the potential to grow at the rate of 175 per cent by AD 2000.

The Problem Flowchart

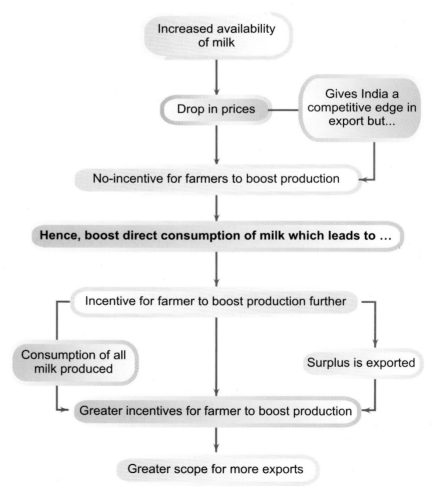

BRAND BUILDING ADVERTISING ■

The Key Concern

A survey among 1,00,000 households in 1995 revealed the low direct consumption of milk. Milk was largely consumed as an intermediary in sweets or as an ingredient in paneer, tea, butter etc.

Consumer Attitudes

```
              ┌──────────────────┐
              │  Good for health │
              └──────────────────┘
                       │
                       ▼
                   ┌───────┐
        ┌──────────│ Milk  │──────────┐
        │          └───────┘          │
        │              │              │
        ▼              │              ▼
┌────────────────┐     │     ┌────────────────┐
│ Rooted in      │     │     │ Integral part  │
│ tradition      │     │     │ of the diet    │
│ and mythology  │     │     │                │
└────────────────┘     │     └────────────────┘
        │              │              │
        │          ┌───────┐          │
        └─────────▶│ But...│◀─────────┘
                   └───────┘
                       │
                       ▼
        ┌────────────────────────────────┐
        │ The young dreary, conservative │
        └────────────────────────────────┘
                       │
                       ▼
                   ┌───────┐
        ┌──────────│ Milk  │──────────┐
        │          └───────┘          │
        ▼                             ▼
┌────────────────┐          ┌────────────────┐
│ The anti-milk  │          │ The health     │
│ lobby: not     │          │ conscious:     │
│ healthy        │          │ fattening      │
└────────────────┘          └────────────────┘
```

The Marketing Objective

It was decided to boost direct consumption of milk to motivate the farmer to produce more milk.

Therefore, though no one needed to be educated about the benefits of milk, people were finding enough reasons not to consume milk directly.

Agency and Client Belief

- The decline in milk consumption was greater among kids/ teens. Milk took a backseat when compared to soft drinks.
- Adults believed that milk was essential for growing children but not for them.

Query Line

Q. Ideation techniques are used in advertising agencies for
- Developing clever ads
- Creating new TV commercials
- New product ideas
- Brand extensions
- All the above

Ans. *Ideation techniques like 'word-association', 'brain storming', 'delphi' are used in agencies for a variety of purposes, not only just by the creative teams looking for visual breakthroughs. Often servicing, planning and media teams spend time ideating on 'how to do things differently.' It could be for a new campaign. A new brand name. A new extension idea. A new TV programme etc.*

Heard-in-the-Agency

"Now we have to be practical. After all with a 40 column centimetres ad you do get four and a half times the exposure."

Communication Task

In this context, the agency believed that educating the consumer about the benefits of milk would make it even more drab and boring.

The communication task was therefore designed to change consumer attitudes towards milk, from being a 'boring, conservative drink' to a 'youthful, exciting and nutritional energy drink'. This entailed the use of communication that would have the look and feel of a soft drink commercial, yet would be firmly rooted in the nutritional values of milk.

Creative Strategy and Execution

The advertising task which sought to bring about a change in consumer attitudes was designed to depict milk as a modern and fashionable drink for today. Although the target group comprised people of all ages, the key target segment was defined as urban, trendsetters, in the age group of 8 to 25 years.

The creative breakthrough was achieved when the writers assigned the task hit upon a unique idea of using the Hindi word for milk '*doodh*' as a musical note. Thus was born the '*doodh doodh*' tune, with '*doodh*' playing the role of the '*sa-re-ga-ma*' and reminding consumers of 'milk', in an interesting manner.

The final creative comprised a 60 second TV film executed with a modern and contemporary treatment, on the lines of a soft drink film. The film showed energetic people of all ages enjoying a glass of milk, with a jingle set to a lively reggae beat extolling the benefits of drinking milk. The jingle was composed with

Hindi-English lyrics, to ride on the popularity of such film songs and music videos.

Media

Television was chosen as the primary medium because of its popularity and the fact that an audio visual medium lends itself to demonstration of 'high energy', 'fun' and 'youthfulness' more vividly.

The strategy initially employed a concentrated burst simultaneously across all media to build up awareness as quickly as possible and used a mix of programmes ske wed towards the 8-14 age group. The campaign ran for a period of 6 months, with a 40 second edit replacing the 60 second film after the first three months.

The first round had a concentrated burst on the main channels i.e. DD1 and DD2 with spots at a fraction of the actual rates. For every paid spot there were four spots given as a bonus to be aired on the same programme. This made the commercial highly visible both in terms of frequency as well as reach. The advertisement got visibility on the Star Plus channel also.

Milk Consumption Today

Any effort to bring about an attitudinal change takes time. A measure of effectiveness of the communication was that the TV commercial was voted by viewers of India's number one satellite channel as one of the best commercials aired on television. The communication has definitely made the youngsters sing the '*doodh doodh*' tune, in addition to the songs of the 'colas'.

Qualitative research threw up findings that revealed a tremendous popularity of the commercial across all age categories. Kids in the age group of 10–12 years were not very resistant in their attitudes towards drinking milk. Mothers took advantage of the popularity of the commercial among their children to make them consume milk.

From the point of view of the industry, per capita availability of milk has gone up from 198 gm/day in 1995 – 96 to 204 gm/day in 1998. Milk consumed through NDDB has gone up from a 100 lakh litres/day in 1995-96 to 113 lakh litres/day in 1998.

Now while the farmers of NDDB set new production records every year, FCB-Ulka takes immense pride in having played a significant role in the wholesome and satisfying experience of propagating the White Revolution.

The entire film set to raggae rap beat as various shots of characters drinking milk.
Jingle: Doodh...Doodh...Doodh

Drink daily once or twice, you will get a tasty surprise.

You will stay fit and fine and live past 99.

Doodh is wonderful, you can drink a glassful everyday.

Doodh is fun in every season. Drink Doodh for healthy reason.

Everywhere there is noise for more milk.

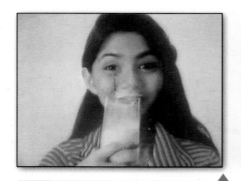

In summer mixing milk with ice, makes milk very nice.

Doodh is wonderful.

Drink one glassful of Doodh.

Poster
NDDB
"Drink a glassful..."

Poster
NDDB
"Piyo glassful..."

Doodh Doodh: Brand Building Tips

Generic selling of a product doesn't necessarily involve dissemination of excessive information. It is often possible to deliver a 'young' 'do-good' message in a likeable, hummable manner, as was done with '*doodh-doodh*'.

GLOSSARY

Advertising : Any paid form of non-personal presentation and promotion of ideas, goods and services by an identified sponsor.

Advertising agency : A professional organisation which plans, creates and places advertising for clients.

Aided-recall method : A method used for testing the memo-rability of advertisements. Some clue that may assist in recalling the brand name is given.

Animatics : A technique for testing less expensive versions of television commercials by producing film or tape of the drawings on the storyboard. In **photomatics**, photographs are used instead of drawings.

Animation : Can refer to animated cartoons or animated objects such as packaging or puppets.

Announcer : The person on radio or television who introduces and describes programmes to the audience.

Appeal : The motive to which an advertisement is directed and which is designed to stir a person towards purchase of the product.

Audience primary : In print, the number of individuals or homes to which the issue was originally circulated may be called primary reader-ship. Or, the people towards whom the editorial content is specifically directed.

Audience secondary : The number of people who are exposed to an issue of a publication but who did not purchase it; also called pass-along readership express the reader's real attitude towards the subject of the research.

Audience : The number and kinds of people classified by their age, sex, composition, income, etc. listening to a radio or television programme.

Audience profile : A demographic description of the people exposed to a medium.

Audio : Sound portion of an advertising film or TV commercial.

Billing	:	Amount of business done by an adver-tising agency.
Bleed	:	To print and trim so that the type or plates run over the edges of the sheet, leaving no margin.
Blow-up	:	Photo enlargement of written, printed or pictorial materials.
Body type	:	The type commonly used for reading matter, as distinguished from display type used in the headlines of advertise-ments. Usually type 14 points in size or smaller.
Boldface type	:	A heavy line type.
Brand	:	The *name* of a product; a set of added values.
Brand development	:	A measurement of a product's percentage of sales as a ratio Index (BDI) (brand sales divided by population).
Brand image	:	The personality of a brand.
Brochure	:	A booklet.
Buried offer	:	An offer of a booklet, sample or infor-mation mentioned in the body copy of an advertisement without the use of a coupon or any emphasis. (Also called hidden offers.)
Campaign	:	A series of advertisements held together by visual similarities, verbal similarities or a similarity of attitude.
Caption	:	The descriptive matter accompanying an illustration or photograph.
Category	:	A measurement of a class of product sales as a ratio.
Development Index	:	Category sales divided by population. **(CDI)**
Centrespread	:	The space occupied by an advertisement on the two facing centre pages of a publication.
Claim	:	Statement about the performance of a prod-uct or service. A **competitive** or **objective claim** must be based upon research, labora-tory testing or other factual evidence. A **subjective claim** does not need support.
Clear	:	To obtain legal permission from respon-sible sources to use a photograph or quotation in an advertisement or to use a certain musical selection in a broadcast.

Column centimetre	:	A unit of measure in a periodical, one centimetre deep and one column wide, whatever the width of the column.
Concept testing	:	Research that helps determine how a product should be positioned.
Consumer promotion	:	Incentives for the consumer to buy the product.
Copy	:	1. The text of an advertisement. 2. Matter for a compositor to set. 3. Any material to be used in the production of a publication.
Copy platform	:	The statement of the basic ideas for an advertising campaign, the designation of the importance of the various selling points to be included in it, and instructions regarding policy in handling any elements of the advertisement.
Copywriter	:	A person who creates the text of advertisements and often the idea, to be visualised as well.
Cost per thousand	:	Cost to reach 1,000 members of a target audience. (**CPP**)
Coverage	:	1. The portion of an area, community or group that may be reached by an advertising medium. 2. The areas in which the radio station or network of stations can be heard according to engineering standards; or the portion of the area, the station or network reached most effectively.
Cropping	:	Trimming part of an illustration to enable the reproduction to fit into a specific space. Cropping is done either to eliminate a non-essential background in an illustration or to change the proportions of the illustration to the desired length and width.
CU	:	Close-up (in television)
Consumer profile	:	An estimate of the demographic characteristics of the people who will buy a brand and the purchase patterns they will produce.

Database	:	A list that goes beyond names and addresses and includes demographic and psychographic information.
Delete	:	"Omit". Used in proof-reading.
Demographics	:	Descriptive facts about a given population group-household income, education, age, sex.
Director	:	The person who writes or rewrites, then casts and rehearses, a television or radio programme and directs the actual performance.
Display	:	1. The quality of attracting attention.
		2. Display type in sizes larger than 14 point. Italics, boldface and Sometimes capitals are used for display; so are hand-drawnletters and scripts.
		3. Display space in newspapers is usually not sold in units of less than 2 column centimetres. There is no such minimum requirement for classified advertisements.
		4. Window display, interior display and counter display are different methods of point-of-purchase advertising.
		5. Open display puts the goods where they can be actually handled and examined by the customer; closed display has the goods in show cases and under glass.
Dissolve	:	The overlapping of an image produced by one camera over that of another and the gradual elimination of the first image.
Double-spread	:	In print, two facing pages used for a single unbroken advertisement, also called double-page spreads.
Dubbing	:	The combining of several sound tracks for recording on film.
Dummy	:	Blank sheets of paper cut and folded to the size of a proposed leaflet, folder, booklet or

book, to indicate weight, shape, size and general appearance. On the pages of the dummy the layouts can be done. A dummy may also be made from the proofs furnished by the printer. Also an empty package or carton used for display purposes.

Duplication : Percentage of people that see the message in more than one media or publication. In direct marketing, appearance of the same name on more than one mailing list.

Effective circulation : The number of people who have a reasonable physical (**outdoor**) opportunity to see a poster. It is defined as half the pedestrians, half the automobiles and one quarter of the public transport passengers passing a poster.

Fade : To diminish or increase the volume of sound on a radio commercial. In film and television, fading in is the gradual appearance of the screen image bright-ening from black to full visibility.

Focus group session : A group of people selected from a target audience, led by a skilled moderator, express their attitudes about a product, service or general topic of interest.

Gross Rating Points (GRPs) : Total of all rating points achieved for a specific schedule or campaign.

Gutter : The space composed of the two inside margins of facing printed pages.

House organ : A publication issued periodically by a firm to further its own interests. Also known as company magazine and company news-letter.

Inserts (FSI—Free Standing Inserts) : In letters of packages, an enclosure usually in the form of a slip bearing an advertise-ment, or in periodicals/newspaper a page printed by the advertiser or for him and inserted into the publication.

Keying an advertisement : Giving an advertisement a code number or letter so that when people respond, the source of the inquiry can be traced. The key

		may be a variation in the address, or number printed in a corner of a coupon.
Kiosk	:	An outdoor structure, usually of standard size, on which sheets of paper bearing advertisements are mounted.
Layout	:	An indication of what the finished print advertisement will look like.
Line extensions	:	Additional products that bear the same brand name and offer the consumer varied options.
Line drawing	:	A drawing where the shading is achieved by variation in size and spacing of lines, not by tone.
Lip synchronisation	:	The method in television and film of having the voice of (**lip-sync**) the per-former recorded as he speaks.
Live	:	In television and radio, a programme which originates at the moment it is produced, in contrast to a programme which is previously taped, filmed or recorded.
Logotype or logo	:	Two or more letters, or a whole word, distinctive style of a name.
Lower case (LC)	:	The small letters in the alphabet, such as these, as distinguished from upper case or capital letters. Named after the printer's type cabinet in which this type was formerly kept.
Mail order	:	A method of selling in which the complete sales transaction is negotiated through advertising and the post and without the use of salesmen. Not to be confused with direct mail advertising.
Make-good	:	A free re-run of an advertisement in which there has been a serious error in repro-duction or transmission.
Make-up of a page	:	The general appearance of a page, the arrangement in which the editorial matter and advertising material are to appear.
Market profile	:	A demographic description of the people or the households of a product's market.

Market research	:	Research carried out to gather facts which are needed to make marketing decisions.
Market share	:	The percentage held by one brand of all products sold in a category.
Marketing	:	An amalgam of those business activities which aid the movement of goods and services from producer to consumer.
Mass medium	:	One which is not directed toward a specific audience and which is widely accepted by all types of people.
Medium	:	The vehicle that carries the advertisement; such as newspaper, magazine, poster, radio, television, outdoor.
Merchandising	:	"The planning involved in marketing the right merchandise or service at the right place, at the right time, in the right quantities and at the right price." (American Marketing Association). Or, the promotion of an advertiser's advertising to his sales force, wholesalers and dealers.
Motivation research	:	Unstructured research (without the use of questionnaires) designed to get a person to express his real attitude towards the subject of the research.
Off camera	:	A television term for an actor whose voice is heard but who does not appear in the commercial.
Overlapping circulation (duplication)	:	The extent to which two or more media duplicate one another in reaching the same prospect. Sometimes this is a desirable feature, providing an immediate cumulative effect.
Page proof	:	A proof of typed matter and plates arranged in pages, as they are to appear finally. Usually made after galley proofs have been shown and corrections made.
Panel	:	A group of people used to secure comparable data on product acceptance, its use and so on, over a period of time; a research facility.
Point, pt	:	The unit of measurement of type, about 1/72 inch in depth. Type is specified by its

point size, as 8 point, 12 point, 24 point, 48 point.

POP (point of purchase)	:	Display advertising or use of other materials in-store.
Primary circulation	:	The residents of households who get a publication (in contrast to pass-along circulation).
Print area	:	The area of a page that type can occupy; the total area of a page minus the margins.
Production department	:	The department responsible for the mechanical production of an advertisement, dealing with printers and engravers. Or, the department responsible for the proper preparation of television or radio programmes.
Progressive proofs	:	A set of photo-engraving proofs in colour, in which the yellow plate is printed on one sheet and the red on another; the yellow and red are then combined; next the blue is printed and a yellow-red-blue com-bination made. The black is printed alone and finally all colours are combined. The sequence varies. In this way the printer matches up his inks while printing colour plates.
Proof	:	An inked impression of composed type or of a plate for inspection or for filing. Or, in engraving and etching, an impression taken to show the condition of the illustration at any stage of the work.
Psychographics	:	Information advertising plus periodic bursts.
Randomisation	:	In consumer research, a method of securing random (unbiased) selection of respondents.
Rating	:	Percentage of homes or individuals tuned in to the average quarter hour or a programme.
Reach	:	The total audience a medium actually covers.
Reach accumulative	:	The total number of homes reached by a medium during a specific time period.

Respondent	:	One who answers a questionnaire or is interviewed in a research study.
Retouching	:	The process of correcting or improving artwork, especially photographs.
Reverse plate	:	An engraving in which whites come out black and vice versa.
Rough	:	The first pencil draft of layout executed in a crude style.
Sales promotion	:	A marketing technique to increase sales, usually through couponing, sweepstakes, contests, gifts or premiums, rebates, in-store displays.
Sample sampling	:	The method of introducing and promoting merchandise by distributing a miniature or full-size trial package of the product free or at a reduced price. Or studying the characteristics of a representative part of an entire market or universe in order to apply to the entire market, the data secured from the miniature part.

A **probability sample** is one in which every member of the universe has a known probability of inclusion.

A **random sample** is a probability sample in which names are picked from a list with a fixed mathematical regularity.

A **stratified quota sample** is one drawn with certain pre-determined restrictions as to the characteristics of the people to be included. An Area Sample (or Stratified Area Sample) is one in which a geographical unit is selected as typical of others in its environment.

In a **judgement sample,** an expert chooses what he considers to be repre-sentative cases suitable for study, based on his experience and knowledge of the field.

A **convenience or batch sample** is one selected from whatever portion of the universe happens to be convenient.

Saturation	: A media pattern of wide coverage and high frequency during a concentrated period of time, designed to achieve maximum impact, coverage or both.
Screen	: The finely cross-ruled sheet used in photomechanical plate-making processes to reproduce the shades of grey present in a continuous tone photograph. Screens come in various rulings, resulting in more, of fewer, "dots" to the square inch on the plate, to match the requirements of different grades and kinds of printing paper.
Self-liquidating	: One for which the cost to an advertiser is fully absorbed by the additional premium paid by the consumer.
Self-mailer	: A direct mail advertisement, folder or booklet that requires no envelope for mailing.
Setting (typesetting)	: Typeset matter to be used as copy for reproduction.
Share-of-Voice	: Number of times the audience sees or hears a brand's (**SOV**) message in relation to all competitive messages.
Silkscreen	: A printing process in which a stencilled design is applied to a screen of silk organdy. A squeezee forces paint or ink through the mesh of the screen to the paper directly beneath.
Slice-of-life	: A commercial that uses a realistic situation and natural language to imitate real life.
Sound effects (SFX)	: Various devices or recordings used in television or radio to produce life-like imitations of sound, such as walking up the stairs, ocean waves, car horns.
Special position	: A desired position in a magazine or newspaper for which the advertiser has to pay extra.
Sponsor	: The firm or individual that pays for talent and broadcasting station time for a radio or television feature : the advertiser on the air.
Stereo	: Duplicate printing plate made by casting molten metal into a matrix or mould of fibre

which has been made under pressure. Lacks the strength and sharpness of detail or an electrotype. Newspapers are printed from stereos.

Storyboard	:	Drawings that depict the action of a commercial, together with a written description of what the viewer will see and hear.
Strategy	:	A plan, preferably in writing, that charts the course of action for marketing your brand.
Super-imposition	:	Showing a trademark of package in a film right over live action.
Target audience	:	Primary prospects sought by an advertiser.
Telemarketing	:	Use of the telephone to sell or buy.
Test marketing	:	Tracking the sales of a new or improved product in one or more cities before marketing it nationally.
Testimonial	:	A commercial that uses real people to endorse a product.
Tone and Manner	:	A projection of your brand's image or personality.
Trade advertising	:	Advertising directed to wholesale or retail merchants or sales agencies through whom the product is sold.
Trade-mark	:	Any device or word that identifies the origin of a product, telling who made it or who sold it. Not to be confused with trade name.
Typeface	:	The style of type selected for the advertisement.
Video	:	In film, the visual reproduction in contrast to its sound or audio.
Vignette	:	A halftone in which the edges (or parts of them) are shaded off gradually to very light grey.
VO (Voice-over)	:	Indication on a storyboard that someone is speaking "off camera."
Wash drawing	:	A brushwork illustration, usually made with diluted India ink or water colour so that, in addition to black and white, it has varying shades of grey like a photograph. Halftones, not line plates are made from wash drawings.

W-O-M **(Word-of-mouth)**	:	Word-of-mouth; The spead of information through word-of-mouth (consumer to consumer).
Zap	:	Obliterating a commercial by fastforwarding with a remote control device.